State Aid Policy in the European Community

A Guide for Practitioners

International Competition Law Series

Volume 16.

The titles published in this series are listed at the end of this volume

State Aid Policy in the European Community

A Guide for Practitioners

by

Phedon Nicolaides
Mihalis Kekelekis
Philip Buyskes

Institut Européen d'Administration Publique
European Institute of Public Administration

KLUWER LAW
INTERNATIONAL

Published by:
Kluwer Law International
P.O. Box 85889
2508 CN The Hague
The Netherlands

Sold and distributed in North, Central and South America by:
Aspen Publishers, Inc.
7201 McKinney Circle
Frederick, MD 21704
USA

Sold and distributed in all other countries by:
Extenza-Turpin Distribution Services
Stratton Business Park
Pegasus Drive
Biggleswade
Bedfordshire SG18 8TQ
United Kingdom

A C.I.P. catalogue record for this book is available from the Library of Congress

Printed on acid-free paper

ISBN 90-411-2394-6

The European Commission supports EIPA through the European Union budget

Printed in The Netherlands

Table of Contents

Note on Authors

Dr Phedon Nicolaides	Professor of Economics, European Institute of Public Administration (EIPA), Maastricht (NL)
Dr Mihalis Kekelekis	Researcher, European Institute of Public Administration (EIPA), Maastricht (NL)
Philip Buyskes	Student Assistant, European Institute of Public Administration (EIPA), Maastricht (NL)

Acknowledgements

We are grateful to Koen Van De Casteele and Winfried Poecherstorfer for their comments on an earlier draft and to Helen Oberg for research assistance.

Preface

This Guide provides a concise overview of the state aid policy of the European Community. It explains the principles on which this policy is based and how it is applied in practice. It also identifies the primary and secondary sources of EC law on state aid and makes references to landmark Commission and Court cases.

The Guide has grown out of seminars on EC state aid law and policy organised during the past few years by the European Institute of Public Administration in Maastricht, the Netherlands. These seminars are intended, among others, for policy-makers and practitioners managing state aid in the public administrations of the EC Member States and its partner countries. As a consequence, the Guide is regularly updated and focuses on those issues that are of practical relevance to the audience in question.

State aid policy is in continuous evolution. Public authorities find new methods of assisting their industries and regions. This means that the Commission and Community Courts constantly need to assess and re-interpret state aid rules, in light of new national policies and determine whether and how they may apply to innovative public measures. At the same time and as integration deepens within the EU, the Community and the Commission are becoming less tolerant of state aid. The rules have been tightened and forms of aid that used to be permitted are no longer authorised.

A "lesson" that can be drawn from the EIPA seminars is that not only should policy makers and practitioners follow closely the various Commission decisions and Court rulings, but they should also monitor practice in other Member States. They have much to learn from the successes and failures of their counterparts in other parts of the Union and from the policies and procedures applied in other Member States. In the field of state aid policy, learning what does not work and what is not allowed is as important as knowing what works and what is allowed.

This book states the law as at 25 March 2005.

Table of Cases

A. COMMISSION DECISIONS

- *Greek Government*, Commission Decision 659/89, OJ L394, 30/12/1989
- *Air France,* Commission Decision 653/94, OJ L254, 31/12/1994
- *Ford Motor Company,* Case N 781/96, OJ C139, 06/05/1997
- *Individual cases under the MEDEA+ scheme*, Case N 702/B/2001, OJ C292, 27/11/2002
- *SFMI-Chronopost*, Commission Decision 365/98, OJ L164, 09/06/1998
- *ESF Elbestahlwerk Feralpi GmbH,* Commission Decision 1999/580/ECSC, OJ L220, 20/08/1999
- *Comité Français d'Organisation*, Commission Decision 12/00, OJ L5, 08/01/2000
- *Compact Discs Albrechts GmbH,* Commission Decision 796/00, OJ L318, 16/12/2000
- *United Kingdom*, Commission Decision 433/03, OJ L149, 17/06/2003
- *France*, Case N 26/2003

B. JUDGEMENTS OF THE COURT OF JUSTICE

- C-30/59, *Steenkolenmijen v High Authority,* 1961 ECR 1
- C-56 and 58/64, *Consten-Grundig,* 1966 ECR 299
- C-6 & 11/69, *Commission v France,* 1969 ECR 523
- C-70/72, *Commission v Germany,* 1973 ECR 813
- C-120/73, *Lorenz v Germany,* 1973 ECR 1471
- C-173/73, *Italy v Commission*, 1974 ECR 709
- C-78/76, *Steinike und Weinlig v Germany,* 1977 ECR 595
- C-61/79, *Amministrazione delle Finance dello Stato v Denkavit Italiana*, 1980 ECR 1205

- C-730/79, *Philip Morris v Commission* 1980 ECR 2671
- C-84/82, *Germany v Commission*, 1984 ECR 1451
- C-323/82, *Intermill v Commission*, 1984 ECR 3809
- C-240/83, *Procureur de la République v ADBHU,* 1985 ECR 531
- C-290/83, *Commission v France*, 1985 ECR 439
- C-234/84, *Belgium v Commission,* 1986 ECR 2263
- C-67/85, 68/85 and 70/85 *Van der Kooy v Commission,* 1988 ECR 219
- C-223/85, *RSV v Commission,* 1987 ECR 4617
- C-57/86, *Greece v Commission,* 1988 ECR 2855
- C-30/87, *Corinne Bodson v SA Pompes funèbres des régions libérées,* 1988 ECR 2479
- C-94/87, *Commission v Germany*, 1989 ECR 175
- C-102/87, *France v Commission,* 1988 ECR 4067
- C-142/87, *Belgium v Commission,* 1990 ECR I-959
- Case C-301/87, *France v Commission*, 1990 ECR I-307
- C-2/88, *Imm. Zwartveld and Others*, 1990 I-3365
- C-303/88, *Italy v Commission,* 1991 ECR I-1433
- C-5/89, *Commission v Germany*, 1990 ECR I-3437
- C-41/90, *Klaus Höfner and Fritz Elser v Macrotron GmbH,* 1991 ECR I-1979
- C-313/90, *CIRFS and Others v Commission,* 1993 ECR I-1125
- C-354/90, *FNCEPA v France*, 1991 ECR I-5505
- C-364/90, *Italy v Commission,* 1993 ECR I-2097
- C-47/91, *Italy v Commission*, 1994 ECR I-4635
- C-72 & 73/91, *Sloman Neptun Schiffahrts AG v Seebetriebsrat Bodo Ziesemer*, 1993 ECR I-887
- C-159/91, *Christian Poucet v Assurances Générales de France and Caisse Mutuelle Regionale du Languedoc – Roussillon*, 1993 ECR I-637
- C-183/91, *Commission v Greece*, 1993 ECR I-3131
- C-189/91, *Kirsammer-Hack v Sidal,* 1993 ECR I-6185
- C-198/91, *William Cook v Commission,* 1993 ECR I-1719
- C-225/91, *Matra v Commission*, 1993 ECR I-3203
- C-320/91, *Paul Corbeau,* 1993 ECR I-2533
- C-387/92, *Banco Exterior de España v Ayuntamiento de Valencia*, 1994 ECR I-877
- C-393/92, *Municipality of Almelo and others v NV Energiebedrijf Ijsslmij,* 1994 ECR I-1477
- C-39/94, *SFEI v La Poste,* 1996 ECR I-3547
- C-159/94, *France v Commission,* 1997 ECR I-5815
- C-311/94, *Ijssel Vliet v Minister van Economische Zaken,* 1996 ECR I-5023

- C-24/95, *Land Rheinland-Pfalz v Alcan Deutschland GmbH,* 1997 ECR I-1591
- C-343/95, *Diego Calì & Figli Srl v Servizi ecologici porto di Genova SpA,* 1997 ECR I-1547
- C-353/95P, *Tierce Ladbroke v Commission,* 1997 ECR I-7007
- C-55/96, *Job Centre coop. arl.*, 1997 ECR I-7119
- C-342/96, *Kingdom of Spain v Commission,* 1999 ECR I-2459
- C-6/97, *Italy v Commission*, 1999 ECR I-2981
- C-174/97P, *FFSA v Commission*, 1998 ECR I-1303
- C-204/97, *Portugal v Commission,* 2001 ECR I-3175
- C-256/97, *DM Transport*, 1999 ECR I-3913
- C-99/98, *Austria v Commission*, 2001 ECR I-1101
- C-351/98, *Spain v Commission*, 2002 ECR I-8031
- C-379/98, *Preussen Elektra AG v Schleswag AG*, 2001 ECR I-2099
- C-261/99, *Commission v France*, 2001 ECR I-2537
- C-382/99, *Netherlands v Commission,* 2002 ECR I-5163
- C-482/99 *French Republic v Commission*, 2002 ECR I-4397
- C-53/00, *Ferring SA v Agence centrale des organismes de sécurité sociale,* 2001 ECR I-9067
- Joined cases C-57/00 and C-61/00, *Freistaat & Volkswagen v Commission,* 2003 ECR I-9975
- C-242/00, *Germany v Commission*, 2002 ECR I-5603
- C-278/00, *Greece v Commission*, 2000 ECR I-8787
- C-280/00, *Altmark Trans,* 2003 ECR I-7747
- C-398/00, *Spain v Commission,* 2002 ECR I-5643
- C-5/01, *Belgium v Commission*, 2002 ECR I-11991
- C-34/01 to C-38/01, *Enirisorse Spa,* not yet reported
- C-83/01 P, C- 93/01 P and C-94/01 P *Chronopost v Ufex and Others,* 2003 ECR I-6993
- C-110/02, *Commission v Council,* not yet reported
- Case C-276/02, *Spain v Commission*, not yet reported

C. JUDGMENTS OF THE COURT OF FIRST INSTANCE

- T-447 & 449/93, *AITEC v Commission*, 1995 ECR II-1971
- T-229/94, *Deutsche Bahn* v *Commission,* 1997 ECR II-1689
- T-266/94, *Skibsværftsforeningen and Others v Commission*, 1996 ECR II-1399
- T-371/94 & T-394/94, *British Airways and Others and British Midland Airways v* Commission, 1998 ECR II-2405

- T-214/95, *Het Vlaamse Gewest v Commission,* 1998 ECR II-717
- T-106/95, *FFSA v Commission,* 1997 ECR II-229
- T-82/96, *ARAP v Commission,* 1999 ECR II-1889
- T-132/96 and T-143/96, *Freistaat Sachsen v Commission,* 1999 ECR II-3663
- T-158/96, *Acciaierie di Bolzano v Commission,* 1999 ECR II-3927
- T-189/97, *Comité d'Entreprise de la Societé Française de Production v Commission,* 1998 ECR II-335
- T-288/97, *Regione Autonoma Friuli Venezia Giulia v Commission,* 2001 ECR II-1169
- T-298/97, 312/97, 313/97, 315/97, 600-607/97, 1/98, 3-6/98, 23/98, *Alzetto Mauro and Others v Commission,* 2000 ECR II-2319
- T-613/97 *Ufex and Others v Commission,* 2000 ECR II-4055
- T-73/98, *Société Chimique Prayon-Rupel SA v Commission,* 2001 ECR II-867
- T-155/98, *SIDE v Commission,* 2002 ECR II-117
- T-36/99, *Lenzing v Commission,* not yet reported
- T-55/99, *Confederación Española de Transporte de Mercancías (CETM) v Commission,* 2000 ECR II-3207
- T-152/99, *HAMSA v Commission,* 2002 ECR II-3049
- T-346/99, T-347/99 and T-348/99, *Territorio Histórico de Álava and Others v Commission,* ECR 2002 II-4259
- T-109/01, *Fleuren Compost BV v Commission,* not yet reported
- T-157/01, *Danske Busvognmænd v Commission,* not yet reported
- T-195/01 and T 207/01, *Government of Gibraltar v Commission,* 2002 ECR II-2309
- T-274/01, *Valmont v Commission,* not yet reported.
- T-291/01, *Dessauer Versogungs und Verkehrsgesellschaft and Others v Commission,* 2002 ECR II-5033

Table of Legislation and Other Official Documents

The following list includes references to the main rules and documents. Recently some documents became obsolete. See the Commission Communication concerning the obsolescence of certain state aid policy documents in OJ C115, 30/4/2004. The website of the DG Competition maintains an updated list.
See: "http://europa.eu.int/comm/competition/state_aid/legislation/"

Provisions of the EC Treaty
Article 36: application of competition to agriculture.
Article 73: state aid for public transport.
Article 86: state aid for providers of services of general economic interest.
Article 87: general incompatibility of state aid with the common market and exceptions.
Articles 88 & 89: provisions on procedures and additional rule making.

Procedural Regulations: Council Regulation 659/99 laying down detailed rules for the application of Art. 93 EC (now Art. 88), OJ L83, 27/03/1999. Commission Regulation 794/2004 on implementing rules and notification, OJ L140, 30/04/2004.

Enabling Regulation (empowers Commission to make implementing regulations): Council Regulation 994/98 on the application of Articles 92 and 93 (now 87 and 88) of the EC Treaty to certain categories of horizontal aid, OJ L142, 14/05/1998.

Commission Regulation 68/2001 on the application of Articles 87 and 88 of the EC Treaty to training aid, OJ L10, 13/01/2001.

Commission Regulation 69/2001 on the application of Articles 87 and 88 of the EC Treaty to de minimis aid, OJ L10, 13/01/2001.

Commission Regulation 70/2001 on the application of Articles 87 and 88 of the EC Treaty to state aid to small and medium-sized enterprises, OJ L10, 13/01/2001.

Commission Regulation 364/2004 amending Regulation 70/2001 as regards the extension of its scope to include aid for research and development, OJ L63, 28/02/2004.

Commission Regulation 2204/2002 on the application of Articles 87 and 88 of the EC Treaty to state aid for employment, OJ L337, 13/12/2002.

Notice on cooperation between national courts and the Commission in the state aid field, OJ C312, 23/11/1995.

Rules applying to horizontal aid

Environmental aid: Guidelines on state aid for environmental protection, OJ C37, 03/02/2001.

Export Credit Insurance: Commission communication concerning the application of Articles 87 and 88 to short-term export credit insurance, OJ C217, 02/08/2001.

Financial Transfers to Public Enterprises: Commission Directive 80/723 on the transparency of financial relations between Member States and public undertakings, OJ L195, 29/07/1980; amended by Commission Directives 85/413, 93/84, and 2000/52 (the latter published in OJ L193, 29/07/2000). Commission Communication to the Member States, OJ C307, 13/11/1993.

Fiscal aid – Direct Business Taxation: Notice on the application of the state aid rules to measures relating to direct business taxation OJ C384, 10/12/1998.

Government Capital Injections: Application of Articles 92 and 93 (now 87 and 88) of the EEC Treaty to public authorities' holdings (Bulletin EC 9-1984).

Public Land Sales: Commission communication concerning aid elements in land sales by public authorities, OJ C209, 10/07/1997.

Regional aid: National ceilings for regional aid coverage under the derogations provided for in Article 92(3)(a) & (c) (now 87(3)(a) & (c)) of the Treaty for the period 2000 to 2006, OJ C165, 21/01/1999. Communication on the links between regional and competition policy reinforcing concentration and mutual consistency, OJ C30, 26/03/1998. Guidelines on National Regional aid, OJ C74, 10/03/1998. Multisectoral Framework on regional aid for large investment projects, OJ C107, 07/04/1998. The framework was extended until 31/12/2003 and then replaced by a new Framework (OJ C70, 19/03/2002) which came into effect on 01/01/2004 and will be valid until 31/12/2009. See also Communication modifying multisectoral framework (no list of sectors with serious overcapacity; transitional measures for motor vehicles and synthetic fibres to continue until 12/2006), OJ C263, 01/11/2003. See finally the Non-Paper of DG Competition for the review of the Regional Aid Guidelines (http://europa.eu.int/comm/competition/state_aid/regional/).

Research and Development aid: Community framework for state aid for Research and Development, OJ C45, 17/12/1996. Commission communication amending the Community framework for state aid for research and development. OJ C48, 13/02/1998.

Rescue and Restructuring aid: Community guidelines on state aid for rescuing and restructuring firms in difficulty, OJ C244, 01/10/2004. See also the new Multisectoral Framework and Rescue and Restructuring aid and Closure aid for the Steel Sector, OJ C70, 19/03/2002, which applies to steel as of August 2002.

Risk Capital: Communication, OJ C235, 21/08/2001. See also the questionnaire for public consultation for the revision of the Communication.

Services of General Economic Interest: Commission communication on services of general interest in Europe, OJ C281, 26/09/1996. Commission communication on the application of the competition rules to the postal sector, OJ C39, 06/02/1998. Commission communication on services of general interest, OJ C17, 19/01/2001. Report to the Laeken European Council on Services of General Interest, COM(2001)598 final, 17/10/2001. "Non-paper" on Services of General Economic Interest, 12/11/2002.
(http://europa.eu.int/comm/competition/state_aid/others/1759_sieg_en.pdf).

State Guarantees: Commission notice on the application of Articles 87 and 88 of the EC Treaty to state aid in the form of guarantees, OJ C71, 11/03/2000.

Rules applying to sectoral aid

Agriculture: Commission Regulation for de minimis aid, OJ L325, 28/10/2004. Regulation 1/2004 on aid to agricultural SMEs, OJ L1, 03/01/2004. Guidelines for state aid in the agricultural sector, OJ C28, 01/02/2000. Guidelines for the examination of state aid to fisheries and aquaculture, OJ C229, 14/09/2004. Council Regulation 26/1962 applying certain rules of competition to production of and trade in agricultural products, OJ 30, 20/04/1962.

Fisheries: Commission Regulation for de minimis aid, OJ L325, 28/10/2004. Commission Regulation 1595/2004 on the application of Articles 87 and 88 of the EC Treaty to State aid to small and medium-sized enterprises active in the production, processing and marketing of fisheries products, OJ L291, 14/09/2004. Guidelines for the examination of state aid to fisheries and aquaculture, OJ C229, 14/09/2004. Guidelines for state aid in the agricultural sector, OJ C28, 01/02/2000.

Air Transport: Application of Articles 92 and 93 (now 87 and 88) of the EC Treaty and Article 61 of the EEA agreement to state aid in the aviation sector, OJ C350, 10/12/1994.

Maritime Transport: Community guidelines on state aid to maritime transport, OJ C13, 17/01/2004.

Road, Rail and Inland Waterway Transport: Council Regulation 543/97 amending Regulation 1107/70 on the granting of aids for transport by rail, road and inland waterway, OJ L84, 26/03/1997. Council Regulation 1107/70 on the granting of aid for transport by rail, road and inland waterway, OJ L130, 15/06/1970. Council Regulation 1191/69 on action by Member States concerning the obligations inherent in the concept of a public service in transport by rail, road and inland waterway, OJ L156, 28/06/1969.
Broadcasting: Communication on aid to public service broadcasting, OJ C320, 15/11/2001.

Coal: Council Regulation 1407/2002. See also Commission Communication, OJ C152, 26/06/2002.

Electricity: Communication on stranded costs, adopted 26/07/2001.

Shipbuilding: Framework on aid to shipbuilding, OJ C317, 30/12/2003.

Recent Policy Developments

2002

New Multisectoral Framework on Regional aid for Large Investment Projects (OJ C70, 19/03/2002)

Extension of R&D Guidelines to 12/2005 (OJ C111, 08/05/2002)

Expiry of Guidelines on aid to Undertakings in Deprived Urban Areas (OJ C119, 22/05/2002)

Notice on the Treatment of Unlawful aid (OJ C119, 22/05/2002)

Regulation on Employment aid 2204/2002 (OJ L337, 13/12/2002)

2003

Launch of a review of guidelines on regional aid after 01/01/2007 (OJ C 110, 08/05/2003)

New form for submission of complaints on state aid (OJ C116, 16/05/2003)

New SME definition (to apply from 01/01/05) (OJ L124, 20/05/2003)

Green Paper on Services of General Interest (COM(2003) 270 final, 21/05/2003)

Exemption regulation in fisheries (July)

Draft exemption regulations (August):

- amendment of training regulation (OJ C190, 12/08/2003)
- inclusion of R&D in SME regulation (OJ C190, 12/08/2003) – adopted 12/2003
- on aid to agricultural SMEs (OJ C194, 15/08/2003) – adopted as Regulation 01/2004

Communication modifying Multi-sectoral Framework (no list of sectors with serious overcapacity; transitional measures for motor vehicles and synthetic fibres to continue until 12/2006) (OJ C263, 01/11/2003)

Communication on professional secrecy in state aid decisions (OJ C297, 09/12/2003)

Framework on aid to shipbuilding replacing Council Regulation 1540/98 (OJ C317, 30/12/2003)

2004

Draft frameworks on lesser amount of state aid and limited effect on trade (01/2004)

Regulation 01/2004 on aid to agricultural SMEs (OJ L1, 3/01/2004)

New guidelines on aid to maritime transport (OJ C13, 17/01/2004)

Regulation 363/2004 modifies training Regulation (OJ L63, 28/02/2004)

Regulation 364/2004 inserts R&D aid in SME Regulation (OJ L64, 28/02/2004)

Communications from the Commission on a Community Framework, a Commission Decision and a Commission Directive on services of general economic interest (March)

Commission Regulation 794/2004 implementing Council Regulation 659/1999 (OJ L140, 21/04/2004)

Commission communication concerning the obsolescence of certain state aid policy documents (OJ C 115, 30/04/2004)

Commission Regulation 1595/2004 on aid to SMEs in fisheries (OJ L291, 14/09/2004)

Guidelines for the examination of state aid to fisheries and aquaculture (OJ C229, 14/09/2004)

Community guidelines on state aid for rescuing and restructuring firms in difficulty (OJ C244, 01/10/2004)

Regulation concerning ''*de minimis*'' aid for the agriculture and fisheries sectors (OJ L325, 28/10/2004)

2005

Revision of the Communication for Risk Capital. Questionnaire for public consultation.

Review of the Regional Aid Guidelines. Non-Paper for discussion from DG Competition

INTRODUCTION

The purpose of this Guide is to provide a concise overview of the state aid policy of the European Community, as reflected in the administrative practice of the European Commission (hereinafter "the Commission") and the case law of the European Court of Justice (hereinafter "the ECJ") and the European Court of First Instance (hereinafter "the CFI").

The importance of this overview cannot be understood fully without taking into account the broader objectives of European Community (hereinafter "EC") competition policy, a basic component of which is the state aid policy.

1. THE OBJECTIVES OF EC COMPETITION POLICY

Competition policy is an instrument for fostering the achievement of the Community's basic objectives. These objectives cover a number of policy areas, such as the establishment of the internal market with no barriers to trade between Member States, the development of a coordinated strategy for public interest goals, such as employment or regional policy; the adjustment to a fast-changing economic environment; the enhancement of industry competitiveness; and the successful implementation of the Monetary Union. Furthermore, Competition policy has to keep pace with the increasing globalisation of trade and the ever increasing rate of technological development.

Despite the multitude of Community objectives, the Treaty of the European Community requires, by laying down Article 3(g) EC, that a system of undistorted competition in the internal market should be ensured. This system can be interpreted as pursuing two distinct objectives: effective competition and market integration.

1.1 Effective competition

Competition policy is one of the major pillars on which the action of the EC in the economic field rests. The EC, and in particular the Commission, have been assigned such broad powers in the competition field, as mentioned below, in order to ensure the achievements of a market economy with free competition. Competition policy promotes consumer welfare, encourages the optimal allocation of resources and grants to economic agents appropriate incentives to pursue productive and innovative efficiency.

An open market economy can only be effectively maintained by preventing collusive agreements between firms or abuses of a dominant position, by ensuring competitive market structures through merger control, and by abolishing those unjustified state subsidies that distort competition by artificially keeping non-viable firms in business.

1.2 Competition policy and market integration

The fundamental objective of the Treaty is the creation of the common market, as stated in Article 2 EC: "(t)he Community shall have as its task, by establishing a common market and an economic and monetary union (…), to promote throughout the Community a harmonious, balanced and sustainable development of economic activities, a high level of employment and of social protection, equality between men and women, sustainable and non-inflationary growth, a high degree of protection and improvement of the quality of the environment, the arising of the standard of living and quality of life, and economic and social cohesion and solidarity among Member States." Article 3 EC lays down the common policies or activities of the Community pursuant to the objectives set out in Article 2 EC.

Competition policy is strictly connected with the creation of the single market. Article 3g EC lays down the requirement that a system of undistorted competition in the internal market should be ensured.

Therefore, competition policy is also an integral part of the common market, with the aim to ensure that the dismantling of the barriers to trade is not replaced by market segmentation introduced by firms. This reasoning was confirmed and developed by the ECJ in the *Consten-Grundig* case, concerning a sole distribution agreement granted by a German supplier to a French distributor, combined with an exclusive trademark right. Particularly the ECJ stated:

"(...) an agreement between producer and distributor which might tend to restore the national divisions in trade between the Member States might be such as to frustrate the most fundamental objectives of the Community. The Treaty, whose preamble and content aim at abolishing the barriers between states, and which in several provisions gives evidence of a stern attitude with regard to their appearance, could not allow undertakings to reconstruct such barriers. Article 85(1) is designed to pursue this aim, even in the case of agreements of undertakings placed at different levels in the economic process."[1]

Consequently, the Community's competition policy supports the completion of the internal market, as laid down in Article 2 EC. "The complementarity between those two policies is also clearly shown by the Community's objective of creating an internal market. On the one hand, the internal market is an essential condition for the development of an efficient and competitive industry. On the other hand, competition policy is an important tool for achieving the goal of, and maintaining, an internal market, in particular via the enforcement of rules ensuring that the regulatory barriers to trade which have been removed are not replaced by private or other public restrictions having the same effect."[2]

2. THE RULES OF COMPETITION IN THE EC

Effective tools are needed in order to contribute efficiently to the achievement of the goals, which are to ensure competitive and integrated markets within the EC.

The Treaty has granted the Council and the Commission powers to achieve that objective. Title VI, chapter 1, and Articles 81 to Article 89 EC provide for the common rules on competition and the means by which these are to be achieved.

Article 81 EC prohibits all agreements and concerted practices between undertakings, which may affect trade between Member States and have the object or effect to restrict competition within the common market. Article 81(3) EC includes a possibility, under certain conditions, for exemptions from the prohibition.

Article 82 EC prohibits the abuse of a dominant position, which may

---

1 Cases 56 and 58/64 1966 ECR 299, at p. 340. See also Nicolaides, Phedon and Van der Klugt, Arianne, *"The Competition Policy of the European Community"*, EIPA, 1994, at p. 9.

2 XXVth Report on Competition Policy 1995, at p. 15.

affect trade between Member States. Article 83 EC refers to the responsibility of the Council of Ministers (hereinafter the "Council") to adopt Regulations and Directives to give effect to the principles set out in Articles 81 and 82 EC, whereas Articles 84 and 85 EC refer to the responsibilities of both the Member States and the Commission during the transitional period before such Regulations and Directives have been enacted.

Articles 86 to 89 EC provide rules governing the activities of Member States in ensuring that public undertakings do not distort competition, as well as rules governing the activities of Member States in providing state aid in whatever form, such as subsidies or special tax advantages, to undertakings (Articles 87, 88, 89 EC).

The need for a common European Competition policy was also recognised in the Treaty establishing the European Coal and Steel Community (ECSC) signed in Paris on 18 April 1951. The Commission had exclusive jurisdiction to decide over these two products, i.e. coal and steel, and the competition rules could not be enforced before the national courts until the Commission had found an infringement (see Appendix XIII on the role of national courts). The ECSC Treaty expired on 23 July 2002.

Finally, Council Regulation (EC) No. 139/2004 of 20 January 2004 on the control of concentrations between undertakings (the EC Merger Regulation),[3] which substitutes Council Regulation (EEC) No. 4064/89 of 21 December 1989 on the control of concentrations between undertakings[4] with effect from 1 May 2004, provides for the mandatory notification of mergers, acquisitions and other kinds of concentration activity that have a Community dimension. The new Merger Regulation forms part of the Commission's endeavour to modernise the legal instruments that constitute the basis of EC competition policy in the run-up to enlargement. The modernisation of competition rules also included, among others, the adoption of Council Regulation (EC) No. 1/2003 of 16 December 2002 on the implementation of the rules on competition laid down in Articles 81 and 82 EC, which became effective on 1 May 2004 as well.[5] The reason for the adoption of this new Regulation was that given the EC's recent enlargement and the continuous globalisation of the economy, a centralised authorisation system, managed by the Commission, would no longer ensure effective application of competition rules and thus the completion of the single market.

In this regard the recent reform contains three central objectives: rigorous

---

3 OJ L24, 29/01/2004.

4 OJ L295, 13/10/1989, with amendments introduced by Council Regulation (EC) No. 1310/1997, OJ L180, 09/07/1997.

5 OJ L1, 04/01/2003.

enforcement of competition law by concentrating on the most important cases involving a real EC interest; effective decentralisation of its application, with the Commission, the national competition authorities and the national courts having concurrent powers to apply EC competition rules and simplification of enforcement procedures, with the ending of the system of notification and authorisation.

Clarification and review of the substantive rules is also an essential pillar in the overall reform process of competition policy, by taking account of the way markets currently operate without losing sight of the integration objectives enshrined in the Treaty.[6] Therefore, new legislation has been proposed and/or adopted in the energy, postal, telecommunications and motor vehicle sectors, pointing towards an even more integrated market, where consumers can benefit from lower prices and improved services.[7]

As for merger control, the relevant EC legislation also needed to be kept up to date, in order to cope with the inevitable increase in merger activity, as a result of the completion of the Monetary Union and the enlargement to a Union of 25. The new Merger Regulation, thus also aims at meeting the need for optimal allocation of enforcement responsibilities.

In the area of state aid, finally, the Commission has recently adopted among others a new regulation on aid to agricultural SMEs,[8] a new regulation for de minimis aid for the agriculture and fisheries sectors,[9] new guidelines for urgency and restructuring aid for companies in difficulty[10] and for maritime transport,[11] draft communications on lesser amount of state aid (LASA) and on aid with limited effect on trade (LET), a proposal for a Community framework for state aid in the form of public service compensation and draft communications on the operations of services of general economic interest (SGEI), as well as a non-paper for discussion for the review of regional aid guidelines.

Of similar importance is the Council procedural regulation for the application of Article 88 EC.[12] This regulation codifies, for the first time, the procedural rules and makes them transparent, thereby increasing legal certainty. The Commission can now force Member States to require interim recovery of illegally granted aid. It also sets time limits for state aid decisions.

---

6 Foreword by Mario Monti, *"XXXII Report on Competition Policy"*, 2002, at p. 5.

7 Directive 2002/39/EC of the European Parliament and of the Council of 10 June 2002 amending Directive 97/67/EC with regard to the further opening to competition of Community postal services, OJ L172, 05/07/2002.

8 OJ L1, 03/01/2004.

9 OJ L325, 28/10/2004.

10 OJ C244, 01/10/2004.

11 OJ C13, 17/01/2004.

3. EC STATE AID CONTROL

State aid control constitutes a basic pillar of EC Competition policy. State intervention influences the way markets operate by favouring certain undertakings, whereas at the same time causing serious damage to other competitors operating in the same and/or different Member States. The Commission's avowed objective is to ensure that state intervention does not interfere with the smooth functioning of the internal market or harm the competitiveness of EU undertakings, as well as to enhance structural reform.[13]

State intervention may, thus come against the objective of a market economy with free and undistorted competition, as enshrined in the Treaty. In order to fulfil this objective of market integration, strict state aid control is needed, in order to maintain a level playing field and ensure that state intervention is kept to a level, where markets and undertakings continue to operate effectively.

In line with the objective of market integration, the EC has made a political commitment to reduce state aid which is thought to remain at too high level. The conclusions of the Lisbon, Stockholm and Barcelona European Councils commit Member States to reduce their overall amount of aid in GDP percentage terms, while redirecting it towards horizontal objectives of Community interest, such as the strengthening of economic and social cohesion, employment, environmental protection, promotion of R&D and development of SMEs.[14] It is also worth noting that both the European Council and the Council of Ministers have urged Member States to grant aid only for the purpose of remedying market failure, to assess the effectiveness of their aid schemes and to avoid undue distortions to competition.[15]

Commission statistics[16] indeed show that the overall level of aid has fallen to € 86 billion in 2001. In terms of sectoral breakdown and the objec-

---

12 Council Regulation (EC) No. 659/1999 of 22 March 1999 laying down detailed rules for the application of Article 88 EC, OJ L83, 27/03/1999 (hereinafter the "Procedural Regulation"). See also the new procedural rules, including a new implementing regulation, adopted by the Commission in April 2004 (Commission Regulation (EC) No. 794/2004 of 21 April 2004 implementing Council Regulation (EC) No. 659/1999 laying down detailed rules for the application of Article 93 of the EC Treaty, OJ L140, 30/04/2004, hereinafter the "Implementing Regulation").

13 XXXII Report on Competition Policy, 2002, at p. 93.

14 Ibid.

15 European Commission (2002), Progress report concerning the reduction and reorientation of State Aid, COM (2002) 555.

16 Statistics can be found in the Surveys of State Aid at: http://europa.eu.int/comm/competition/state_aid/others/#discuss and in the State Aid Scoreboard, which is regularly updated and can be accessed at: http://europa.eu.int/comm/competition/state_aid/scoreboard.

tives of state aid, a comparison of recent periods also shows a reduction in the amount of state aid that is granted to specific industries:

Overall average annual national aid in the EC: (1993 / 2002)

Overall aid: € 112 bn / € 86 bn (2001)
Of which, aid to manufacturing & services: € 60 bn / € 34 bn
(remaining aid was granted to agriculture, fisheries and transport)

State aid to manufacturing & services in the EC: (1994 / 2002)

Horizontal objectives: 31% / 70%
Particular sectors and rescue & restructuring: 11% / 30%
Regional objectives: 58% / 25%

Country	State Aid in 2002 (euro billion)			
	Total [less railways]	Total [less agric. fish. transport]	Total [less railways as % GDP]	Total [less agric. fish. transp. as % GDP]
EU	48.8	34.0	0.56	0.39
A	1.3	0.5	0.63	0.21
B	1.3	0.9	0.53	0.37
DK	1.6	1.3	0.92	0.72
D	13.3	11.4	0.65	0.56
E	4.3	3.5	0.68	0.55
FIN	1.7	0.2	1.28	0.17
F	9.7	6.2	0.66	0.42
GR	0.7	0.4	0.52	0.31
I	6.0	4.5	0.50	0.38
IRL	1.0	0.5	0.85	0.45
L	0.1	0.06	0.41	0.26
NL	1.9	0.8	0.46	0.19
P	1.0	0.6	0.83	0.55

Country	State Aid in 2002 (euro billion)			
	Total [less railways]	Total [less agric. fish. transport]	Total [less railways as % GDP]	Total [less agric. fish. transp. as % GDP]
S	1.0	0.4	0.39	0.16
UK	3.9	2.6	0.25	0.17

CHAPTER I

The Application of EC Competition Rules to State Aid

1. STATE AID IN THE EC TREATY

The further we progress towards full market integration the more harmful are distortions of competition. On the one hand, aid may be provided to undertakings in order, for example, to meet the needs of new technological developments, and this may be considered to be beneficial to the economy.[17] On the other hand however, the beneficial effects of liberalisation may be undermined by state interventions, which weaken effective competition and prevent the achievement of market integration.

State aid is thus considered to be in principle incompatible with the common market. Article 87(1) EC declares any aid which distorts competition and affects trade between Member States to be incompatible with the common market, unless the Treaty dictates otherwise. This qualification implies that certain exceptions are possible to this general prohibition of state aid. In this respect, the second and third paragraphs of Article 87 define certain categories of aid that are either compatible or may be declared compatible with the common market. It is the exclusive responsibility of the Commission to examine the compatibility of state aid with the common market. It is important, in this regard, to point out that we are referring to aid awarded by the public authorities of the Member States, following the respective national rules of substance and procedure. National rules governing the award of state aid are not harmonised. However, although the European Commission cannot intervene with the national process of award, it supervises the award to ensure that competition in the common market is not distorted either by the aid itself or procedures that may discriminate against certain firms.[18]

---

17 Eleventh Report on Competition Policy (1981), at p. 179.

Article 88 EC defines the procedure on the basis of which Member States are required to notify all new state aid (in schemes or individual awards) or amendments to existing state aid schemes to the Commission for assessment. State aid cannot be granted or put into effect unless it has been approved or deemed to have been approved by the Commission. The procedure of Article 88 EC has been extended and elaborated by Council Regulation 659/99 laying down detailed rules for the application of Article 93 EC (now Article 88).

2. ARTICLE 87(1) EC: AID INCOMPATIBLE WITH THE COMMON MARKET

State aid policy in the European Community is laid down in Article 87(1) EC, which provides that:

> "Save as otherwise in this Treaty, any aid granted by a Member State or through state resources in any form whatsoever which distorts or threatens to distort competition by favouring certain undertakings or the production of certain goods shall, in so far as it affects trade between Member States, be incompatible with the common market."

This wording indicates that state aid is in principle prohibited within the common market. Article 87(1) EC does not present a concrete definition of the concept of state aid by reference to its cause or objective but rather defines it by reference to its effect.[19] The meaning of aid is derived from the interpretation of Article 87 EC in the rulings of the Community Courts and the decisions of the Commission. Thus, a measure of public support is classified as state aid only if the conditions defined in that paragraph are all satisfied. Alternatively, not all measures of public support, even those that may involve public subsidies, are necessarily classified as state aid.

The five conditions that must all hold are the following:

(a) aid must be granted by the state or through state resources;
(b) this aid must confer an advantage to the recipients;
(c) the advantage must favour certain (selected) undertakings or economic activities;
(d) aid must affect trade between Member States; and
(e) aid must distort competition in the common market.

---

18 Connor Quigley & Anthony M. Collins, *EC State Aid Law and Policy*, 2003, Hart Publishing, at p. 2.
19 Case 30/59, *Steenkolenmijnen v High Authority*, 1961 ECR 1, at p. 19.

However, there are at least three situations, as the Advocate-General commented in the case *Italy v Commission*, where despite the presence of the aforementioned factors, the intervention does not constitute state aid in the strict sense of the term, namely:

"(a) where the state conducts itself like a private commercial operator;[20]
(b) where the state is discharging obligations of a civil nature such as the obligation to make reparation for loss and damage or to pay back sums unduly required;[21] and
(c) where the exceptional measure forms part of a general system – of taxation or social security, for example – and is justified by the nature of general scheme of the system."[22,23]

2.1 Aid by Member States or through state resources

Article 87(1) EC refers to aid granted "by a Member State or through state resources." "Member States" includes central governments and its ministries or departments, regional and local governments or councils. "State resources," on the other hand, refers to public or private bodies designated or established by the state and which use resources which belong to the state or are controlled by the state.[24] Any aid given by private entities (e.g. privately-owned companies) is not considered to be state aid and, thus, fall outside the scope of Article 87 EC. However, a private company, whose board is appointed or otherwise controlled by the state would also be considered as part of the state and would, therefore, fall within the scope of Article 87 EC.[25]

This distinction was thought by some to suggest that the concept of aid was wider than mere transfer of monetary resources and in addition covered advantages of regulatory nature. It is now clear from the case law that only advantages granted directly or indirectly through state resources are to be considered aid within the meaning of Article 87 (1) EC and that the advantages of pure regulatory nature are excluded from that Article.[26] Article 87(1) EC thus

---

20 Case C-301/87, *France v Commission*, 1990 ECR I-307, at para. 39.
21 Case C-61/79, *Amministrazione delle Finance dello Stato v Denkavit Italiana*, 1980 ECR 1205, at para. 31.
22 Case C-173/73, *Italy v Commission*, 1974 ECR 709, at point 13.
23 Opinion of the A.G. on Case C-6/97, *Italy v Commission*, 1999 ECR I-2981.
24 Case C-72-73/91, *Sloman Neptun Schiffahrts AG v Seebetriebsrat Bodo Ziesemer*, 1993 ECR I-887, at para. 19.
25 Case C-482/99 *French Republic v Commission*, 2002 ECR I-4397.
26 Case C-379/98, *Preussen Elektra AG v Schleswag AG*, 2001 ECR I-2099, at para. 58.

applies to all state aid and covers all transfer of resources without being necessary to make a distinction whether the aid is granted by the agents of the state or enterprises controlled by the state or by the state itself.[27]

Two questions need to be answered for applying Article 87(1) EC with regard to the definition of aid granted by a Member State or through state resources:

a) What are "state resources," and
b) Is the decision to transfer these state resources "imputable" to the state?

According to the opinion of A.G. Jacobs in the *Stardust Marine* case, state resources are those resources which are directly or indirectly under the control or in other words at the disposal of the state.[28] This definition was followed in the judgement of the ECJ, which stated that:

> "The state is perfectly capable, by exercising its dominant influence over such undertakings, of directing the use of their resources in order, as occasion arises, to finance specific advantages in favour of other undertakings."[29]

However, state resources can be considered as state aid only if their granting is imputable to the state. The advantage conferred by the state in order to be counted as aid must be supported by state resources in terms of actual or potential financial liabilities. In other words, aid must have a budgetary consequence for the government. This entails that aid, in the meaning of Article 87 EC, may be defined as whatever the government gives from its own resources or fails to receive from what is owed to it. ECJ has so far used a pragmatic approach and established a number of indicators relevant in concluding whether the activities of the undertakings can be imputed to the state for the purposes of Article 87(1) EC.

Thus, in the *Van der Kooy* case the ECJ concluded that the measure was attributed to the state because the public undertakings in question had to comply with directives issued by a ministerial committee.[30] More broadly, the fact that a body cannot decide without taking into account the requirements of public authorities has been held to constitute an indicator of imputability.[31]

On the other hand, regarding case law where imputability was not found, in a landmark case concerning Germany's international Shipping Register,

---

27 Case C-290/83, *Commission v France*, 1985 ECR 439, at para. 14.
28 Opinion of A.G. on Case C-482/99 *French Republic v Commission*, at para. 39.
29 Case C-482/99 *French Republic v Commission*, 2002 ECR I-4397, at para. 38.
30 Joined Cases C-67/85, 68/85 and 70/85 *Van der Kooy v Commission*, 1988 ECR 219, at para. 55.

German rules enabled the contracts of employment concluded with seafarers from non-member countries and having no permanent residence in Germany, to be subjected to less favourable working conditions and lower rates of pay than resident seafarers. Those rules were alleged by the trade unions to be tantamount to illegal aid. However, the ECJ ruled that the system applicable by the ship register did not constitute state aid, as it did not seek to create an advantage that would be an additional budgetary burden to the state. There was no transfer of state resources and, therefore, the scheme fell outside the scope of Article 87 EC.[32]

The same holds when the transfer of resources takes place between private undertakings. In the recent *Preussen Elektra* case, the ECJ ruled that there was no impact on the public budget and any indirect reduction of tax revenues was an inherent feature of the scheme.[33]

This means that regulatory or administrative measures are not considered to be aid even if they confer a commercial advantage to certain undertakings. Such measures do not normally have a budgetary effect for the state. Even though, for example, relaxation of anti-pollution restrictions could reduce the operating costs of an industry and, therefore, could give it a substantial advantage over its competitors, it is not state aid covered by Article 87 EC. It could, however, infringe other provisions of the Treaty. For instance, it may be contrary to the various environmental directives. In addition, the granting by the state of an advantage to a company in the form of an exclusive right to operate, for example, infrastructural facilities at special financial terms confers an advantage that may infringe Articles 82 and 86 EC and/or Community rules on public procurement.

Other regulatory measures that have been found not to constitute state aid are, for example, the exclusion of certain enterprises from labour regulations (e.g. easier dismissal of workers) and protection of certain type of enterprises

---

31 Ibid. In the *Stardust Marine* case the ECJ added a number of other indicators that might, in certain circumstances be relevant in concluding for imputability: "the level of the undertaking's integration into the structures of the public administration; the nature of its activities and the exercise of the latter on the market in normal conditions of competition with private operators; the legal status of the undertaking (...); the intensity of the supervision (...); and any other indicator showing, in the particular case, an involvement by the public authorities in the adoption of a measure or the unlikelihood of their not being involved, having regard also to the compass of the measure, its content or the conditions which it contains" (cited above at No. 25, at para. 56).

32 Case C-72 & 73/91, *Sloman Neptun Schiffarts AG v Seebetriebsrat Bodo Ziesemer*, 1993 ECR I-887 (cited above at No. 24).

33 Case C-379/98, *Preussen Elektra AG v Schleswag AG* (cited above at No. 26). See also *Stardust Marine* case (cited above at No. 25, at para. 52), where the ECJ stated that "it is also necessary to examine whether the public authorities must be regarded as having been involved, in one way or another, in the adoption of those measures."

from creditors.

In summary, the following steps may be followed in determining whether the State is the source of aid:

Stages	Questions	Outcome
I	Does the measure have an impact on the budget of a public authority or does it affect the assets or liabilities of a public authority?	If the answer is yes, there is transfer of public resources. If the answer is no, go to Stage II.
II	Does the measure involve transfers from a fund which is controlled by a public authority?	If the answer is yes, there is transfer of public resources. If the answer is no, go to Stage III.
III	Is the measure undertaken by an agent of the state or an undertaking controlled by the state and can the measure be attributed to the decision of a public authority?	If the answer is yes, there is transfer of public resources. If the answer is no, there is no transfer of public resources. Either the resources are private or the measure is regulatory.

2.2 Recipients of aid

The recipients of aid must be "undertakings" which are natural or legal persons engaging in economic activities. An undertaking for the purposes of Article 87 EC can be a professional self-employed person (such as a lawyer or accountant), a partnership, a private company, a group of companies,[34] or a public company wholly or partially owned or controlled by the state. Article 87 EC also applies to aid granted to undertakings located in another Member State.[35]

The concept of an undertaking is not defined anywhere in the Treaty. It refers broadly to any natural or legal person, regardless of legal status and

[34] Case C-303/88, *Italy v Commission,* 1991 ECR I-1433, concerning aid granted to ENI, a state holding company, owning the Lanerossi group of companies. In this case the ECJ stated that the Commission was entitled to regard the funds provided by ENI through Lanerossi to four of its subsidiaries as State aid, without it being necessary to establish that the capital funds received by ENI from the Italian Government were specifically intended to make up losses of the subsidiaries. It was sufficient to observe that in any event the receipt of the capital funds enabled ENI to release other resources to make up for the losses of the subsidiaries (para. 14).

[35] Case C-353/95P, *Tierce Ladbroke v Commission,* 1997 ECR I-7007

means of being financed, who carries out economic activities of certain regularity and duration and which could be done for remuneration.

An essential aspect of an undertaking is the ability to make independent economic or commercial decisions. Therefore, groups of related companies that cannot individually pursue an autonomous business strategy are considered to constitute a single undertaking. In the *Bodson* case the ECJ pointed out that Article 81 EC is not concerned with agreements or concerted practices between firms forming a single economic unit.[36] Anti-competitive behaviour on the part of an undertaking within an economic unit should therefore be considered in the light of Article 82 EC. This indicates that an economic unit should be regarded as one undertaking falling under Article 81 EC. By implication and as will be explained later on, agents acting on behalf of a principal are not separate undertakings, even though they may have a separate legal personality.

The concept of an undertaking is not restricted by size, means of financing, legal status or possible government ownership. Associations of companies thus and government agencies may also be undertakings for the purposes of competition policy.

Furthermore, there is no need for the companies to always pursue profitable activities, in order to be considered as undertakings. In *Höfner*[37] and *Job Centre,*[38] the ECJ ruled that a public employment agency was an undertaking because employment procurement has always been an economic activity pursued for profit (commercial reasons), even if in that particular case it was not done for the purpose of profit. By contrast, the charging of fees does not turn an entity into an undertaking. An anti-pollution monitoring agency in the port of Genoa was found not to be an undertaking, even though it charged an obligatory fee to vessels, the reason being that its services were not economic but mandated in the context of public policy.[39]

Examples of entities which have been found to be undertakings:

- private and public (quoted on stock exchange) companies;
- professional persons;
- the new money transfer system for the Euro, "Target"; it falls within the scope of Article 81 (1) EC for transactions involving commercial financial institutions but it is outside the scope of Article 81 (1) EC for transactions involving central banks;
- the European Broadcasting Union (which runs Eurovision);

---

[36] Case C-30/87, *Corinne Bodson v SA Pompes funèbres des régions libérés,* 1988 ECR 2479.

[37] Case C-41/90, *Klaus Höfner and Fritz Elser v Macrotron GmbH,* 1991 ECR I-1979.

[38] Case C-55/96, *Job Centre coop. arl.*, 1997 ECR I-7119.

[39] Case C-343/95, *Diego Calí & Figli Srl v Servizi ecologici porto di Genova SpA*, 1997 ECR I-1547;

- entities managing pensions based on voluntary contributions;
- Comité Français d'Organisation, which organised the 1998 Football World Cup.[40]

Examples of entities which have been found not to be undertakings:

- public authorities in exercising their regulatory role are not undertakings; e.g. local authorities regulating provision of funeral services by awarding licences to private companies;[41]
- social security bodies administering funds from compulsory contributions based on the principle of national solidarity.[42]
- persons in the employment of a single employer (they do not have commercial decision–making autonomy, they form part of an economic unit, which is the firm employing them), as well as their representatives, i.e. trade unions.
- organisations such as groups promoting culture and art, schools offering compulsory education, and other entities providing services to the general public on a non-commercial basis (e.g. weather information).

In summary, the following steps may be followed in determining whether the recipient entity is an undertaking:

Stages	Questions	Outcome
I	Is the recipient acting in an official capacity or as a public authority?	If the answer is yes, the recipient is not an undertaking. If the answer is no, go to Stage II.
II	Does the recipient offer goods or services for which there is a market where parties make offers to others on remuneration?	If the answer is no, the recipient is not an undertaking. If the answer is yes, go to Stage III.
III	Do the activities of the recipient involve transactions of unequal value between what it offers and what it receives or are the transactions mandated by the state?	If the answer is yes, the recipient is not an undertaking. If the answer is no, the recipient is an undertaking?

---

40 Commission Decision 2000/12, OJ L5, 08/01/2000.

41 Case C-30/87, *Corinne Bodson v SA Pompes funèbres des régions libérées,* 1988 ECR 2479.

42 Case C-159/91, *Christian Poucet v Assurances Generales de France and Caisse Mutuelle Regionaledu Languedoc – Roussillon*, 1993 ECR I-0637.

2.3 Advantage granted

State aid, therefore, has been interpreted by the Commission and the Community Courts to include any transfer of state resources that favours one or more undertakings, resulting in a competitive advantage that could not have been obtained under normal market conditions, whereas the recipient(s) of the aid do not have to provide anything in return. Aid itself is any relief from the expenses, which are normally borne by undertakings in their daily operations. As the CFI stated:

> "Article 87(1) EC is aimed merely at prohibiting advantages for certain undertakings and the concept of aid covers only measures which lighten the burdens normally assumed in an undertaking's budget and which are to be regarded as an economic advantage which the recipient undertaking would not have obtained under normal market conditions."[43]

Article 87(1) EC applies to aid in any form. The concept of aid is very wide and includes any advantage of monetary nature conferred by the state or the agents of the state, which would not have otherwise been enjoyed by the recipient or otherwise favoured companies or sectors. Such advantages encompass not only grants, subsidies, loans or guarantees actually given by the state, but also anything owed to the state, which the latter fails to collect or receive, such as taxes, social security payments, interest on loans and dividends on invested public capital, as well as anything that the state gives up without objective reason such as products and services it sells at excessively low prices and anything the state gives away without objective reason such as products and services it purchases at excessively high prices.

The actual form of the aid or the intentions and the formal objectives of the public policies of the authority granting the aid, are irrelevant for the purposes of Article 87(1) EC. Even if a policy has no formal objective of conferring an advantage or assisting an undertaking, its application may still inadvertently favour certain undertakings over others. Article 87(1) EC bans aid according to its actual or potential effects, rather than the declared intentions of the granting authority.[44]

The Advocate-General in the *Italy v Commission* case puts it very succinctly:

---

43 Case T-157/01, *Danske Busvognmænd v Commission*, at para. 57. The implication from this case was that lightening of "abnormal" burdens is not aid. Combus, a bus company, was compensated by the Danish government for its extra costs of employing civil servants after it was privatised.

44 Case C-173/73, *Italy v Commission* (cited above at No. 22).

"Since 1961, the Court of Justice has consistently interpreted the concept of aid solely by reference to its effects (e.g. C-30/59): the decisive criterion is not the form that the intervention takes, nor of course, its legal nature or the aim it pursues (e.g. C-173/73) but the result to which it leads. Any intervention which gives rise to an economic advantage, accompanied by a correlative decrease in state resources, and benefits a particular undertaking or sector of production, is in principle state aid for the purposes of Article (87) of the Treaty"[45]

It follows from the EC definition of state aid that this notion is very wide. It includes a large variety of measures, such as:

- grants;
- loans at below-market rates of interest from the state; interest subsidies;
- guarantees by the state for which the beneficiary does not pay a market fee;
- tax advantages: tax base reductions, tax deferment, tax cancellation, tax rate reduction, tax exemptions;
- reductions of social security contributions;
- provision of goods and services by the state at below-market prices;
- sale of land at below-market price by the state;
- purchase of goods and services by the state at above-market prices;
- capital injections which are not in conformity with the market economy investor principle (lower expected return than what a private investor would demand at similar market conditions and risk).[46]

There have been lengthy discussions as to whether a public support measure that compensates the recipients for the extra costs of obligations to provide services in the general economic interest imposed by the state can be considered as conferring advantage in the meaning of Article 87(1) EC. This issue however is discussed in detail below, when considering the exceptions from Article 87(1) EC.

---

45 Opinion of the A.G. on Case C-6/97, *Italy v Commission* (cited above at No. 23 at para. 22).

46 For the manufacturing sector the instruments that were most frequently used in the EU during the 1996-1998 period were grants (58%), tax exemptions (23%) and soft loans (11%).These figures are provided in the Eighth Survey on State Aid in the European Union. Aid in the form of state equity participation, represents only 4% of all aid to the manufacturing sector granted in the European Union. Tax deferrals – mainly accelerated depreciation and the constitution of tax-free reserves – as well as guarantees are not often used. The latest edition of the State Aid Scoreboard (Spring 2003) indicates that in the period 1999-2001 grants accounted for 63% of all aid to manufacturing, tax exemptions 26%, soft loans 7% and guarantees 3%.

2.3.1 Private investor principle

To be able to assess when the actions of a government indirectly constitute state aid by conferring an advantage to certain undertakings, the Commission has developed the "private investor" principle. In order to establish the existence of aid, the Commission would compare the situation in question under the prevailing market conditions with the behaviour of private investors in similar circumstances. The ECJ has also held in this regard that, in order to determine whether a state measure constitutes aid for the purposes of Article 87(1) EC, it is necessary to establish whether the recipient undertaking receives an economic advantage, which it would not have obtained under normal conditions.[47] According to this principle, public authorities may give loans, guarantees, inject capital and otherwise be involved in commercial ventures, but at the same time they must behave in the same way as a private investor would behave in similar circumstances. So there is aid when, for example, the government invests in a company that has suffered financial losses and which cannot survive without public money. The same applies when a government buys shares in a company and for years it receives no dividend and no return on its capital. On the other hand, repayment agreements with public creditors are considered to fall outside Article 87(1) EC, if private creditors would have taken the same decision in order to recover the sums due to them.[48]

However, a question can be raised as to what happens when there are no similar circumstances or comparable market conditions? That was the situation in the *Chronopost* case, where La Poste, a legal monopolist in the ordinary mail sector in France, was found to be in a situation very different from that of a private undertaking acting under normal market conditions, given that it was at the time operating in a market network with substantial infrastructures and resources, which would never had been created by a private undertaking. As a result, in the absence of any possibility of comparing the situation with that of a private group of undertakings not operating in a reserved sector, the ECJ put aside the judgement of the CFI and upheld the Commission's decision excluding the existence of State aid in the provision of logistical and commercial assistance by La Poste to Chronoposte.[49] In such cases, "normal market conditions", which are necessarily hypothetical, must be assessed by reference to the objective and verifiable elements which are available[50]. For example, if a sold land had been valued by independent sur-

---

47 Case C-39/94, *SFEI v La Poste,* 1996 ECR I-3547, at para. 60.

48 Case C-342/96, *Kingdom of Spain v Commission,* 1999 ECR I-2459.

49 Joined Cases C-83/01 P, C-93/01 P and C-94/01 P, *Chronopost v Ufex and Others,* 2003 ECR I-6993.

50 Ibid. at para. 38.

veyors and the price for which it was sold was higher than that valuation, the sale would not be found to have included aid. If, on the other hand, a public investment in the steel mill is accompanied by substantial investment on the same terms by one or more private investors, then it is unlikely that the injection of capital constitutes aid. The point that needs to be borne in mind is that the Commission always seeks to establish whether government action can be justified on objective commercial criteria.

2.3.2 Public creditor principle

The failure or unwillingness of a public authority to demand money owed to it is also a form of state aid. As the Community courts have repeatedly stated, the concept of aid is wider than that of a subsidy because it embraces not only positive benefits, such as the subsidies themselves, but also measures, which in various forms mitigate the normal burdens on the budget of an undertaking.[51] For example, when a public authority tolerates late payment of money owed to it by undertakings, it mitigates their financial burden and places those undertakings in an advantageous position *vis-à-vis* their competitors.[52] Public authorities, therefore, have to pursue their debtors with the same vigour as that of a private creditor.[53]

In practice when the courts assess the application of the public creditor, they resort to the simpler criterion of trying to determine whether the public authority concerned pursued all legally possible options and whether it acted promptly. These issues are illustrated well in the two most recent cases concerning *Lenzing v Commission*,[54] and *Spain v Commission*,[55] where the courts annulled the contested Commission Decisions, but on different grounds.

In *Spain v Commission*, the Court of Justice (ECJ) examined a Commission Decision which had found that the Spanish authorities had not acted as a private creditor. The undertaking concerned had not paid taxes and social security for three years before the Spanish authorities agreed to write-off two thirds of the debt and reschedule repayment of the rest over a ten-year period. After that agreement, the undertaking continued to fail to pay what the State owed and a year later the authorities began seizing its property. Eventually, the agreement was suspended a year afterwards.

---

51 See, inter alia, Case 30/59, *De Gezamenlijke Steenkolenmijnen Limburg v High Authority* (cited above at no. 19); Case C-387/92, *Banco Exterior de España* 1994 ECR I-877; C-256/97, DM Transport, 1999 ECR I-3913; C-5/01, *Belgium v Commission*, 2002 ECR I-11991.

52 See *DM Transport*, ibid.

53 See Case C-342/96, *Spain v Commission*, (cited above at no. 48).

54 Case T-36/99, not yet reported.

55 Case C-276/02, not yet reported.

The ECJ accepted the arguments of Spain that the authorities used all the options that were legally available to them culminating in confiscation of property and eventual closure of the company. There was also some evidence that the authorities tried to seize property earlier. It seems that these draconian measures were sufficient to persuade the ECJ that the authorities acted as a private creditor would have acted in a similar situation, and therefore it annulled the Commission Decision.

In the case *Lenzing v Commission*, the Spanish authorities were dictated by law to fix only a statutory rate of interest on the outstanding debt. The statutory rate was lower than the market rate, but this difference in itself is not sufficient to prove the existence of state aid. This is because a creditor would not apply the same rate as an investor who seeks to maximise profits. A creditor may accept a lower rate so as to minimise losses.[56]

However, the relevant Spanish law did not stipulate the amount of repayments, the number of instalments or the length of the repayment period. In this case, the Court of First Instance (CFI) did recognise the discretion of the authorities on these matters and concluded that that discretion was sufficient to convert actions dictated by law into a form of state aid. In particular, the CFI explicitly referred to the fact that the Spanish authorities had tolerated non-payment of social security contributions for several years. In fact, the CFI rejected a Spanish argument that there was no state aid because the actions of the authorities were not arbitrary. The CFI made a distinction, significant in this context, between arbitrariness and discretion.

Then the CFI went on to state that "[...] in order for the advantages described above to be capable of being classified as aid for the purposes of Article 87(1) EC, it must still be established that [the undertaking in question] could not have obtained them under normal market conditions [...]. More specifically, the Court must consider whether the Commission made a manifest error in concluding that the Social Security Fund and Fogasa acted in the same way as a hypothetical private creditor in so far as possible, the same situation *vis-à-vis* its debtor as those two bodies".[57] At the end, the CFI found that the Commission had not proven that the Spanish authorities had acted as a private creditor in allowing accumulation of debt in the first place, then in agreeing to reschedule that debt over a ten-year period and finally in allowing again the undertaking not to honour the rescheduling agreement. Consequently, it annulled the Commission Decision that had found that there was no state aid in the actions of those authorities.

---

56 *Spain v Commission* (Tubacex) (cited above at no. 48).

57 Cited above at No. 54, para. 149.

2.3.3 Objective justification

What happens when there is no obvious market benchmark against which to compare prices or interest rates in order to detect the existence or not of a hidden subsidy? How can aid be objectively justified by the prevailing market conditions? This was the central point of contention in a celebrated case involving a public gas utility in the Netherlands in the early 1980s. The Commission contended that Gasunie, the gas utility in question, gave aid to undertakings engaged in greenhouse horticulture by lowering the tariffs it charged for supplying gas to them. Gasunie argued that those undertakings were energy-intensive businesses and its tariff structure simply reflected discounts for large purchases and also incentives for them not to convert their heating plants to coal. The Commission also claimed that, irrespective of the Gasunie's motives, the lower tariff for horticulture was state aid because it was not available to other large users of gas in other industries. Eventually, the Commission's decision (85/215) was challenged before the ECJ.

The ruling of the ECJ is instructive. It first found that objective differentiation in the tariff structure among distinct classes of customers on the basis of sound economic reasoning is an acceptable commercial practice. There is no aid, for example, in offering discounts to large users of gas. The ECJ also found acceptable the aim of Gasunie to maintain low tariffs so as to keep its customers from converting to coal. The question at issue was whether Gasunie, "unlike an ordinary economic agent," acted to "confer a pecuniary advantage on energy consumers, forgoing the profit which it could normally realise."

The ECJ concluded that the level of the tariff charged by Gasunie to greenhouses could not be objectively justified on economic grounds. The difference between the low tariff and the immediately higher was much bigger than the cost of conversion of heating plants to coal and the price of coal. The tariff for gas to horticulture was lower than what was necessary to prevent conversion and retain them as customers of Gasunie.[58]

Hence, there is no element of state aid when (a) price differentials are part of an integral tariff system and can be justified on an objective basis (e.g. large purchases, long-term contracts, payments in cash) and (b) price reductions or discounts are made as a necessary response to commercial pressure (e.g. retaining customer loyalty).

In summary, the following steps may be followed in determining whether a state measure confers an advantage:

---

[58] Joined cases 67/85, 68/85 and 70/85, *Van der Kooy v Commission* (cited above at No. 30).

Stages	Questions	Outcome
The State procures or sells goods and services		
I	Are the transactions open and through competitive processes?	If the answer is yes, there is no advantage. If the answer is no, go as appropriate to Stage II or III.
The State acts as a private investor or private creditor		
II	Is the investment or credit granted at market conditions [ignoring public policy concerns]?	If the answer is yes, there is no advantage for beneficiary undertaking. If the answer is no, there is advantage for beneficiary undertaking.
The State acts as a public authority		
III	Does the measure reduce normal or inherent costs of recipient?	If the answer is yes, go to Stage IV. If the answer is no, examine why the costs are abnormal. If the state has caused the costs, perhaps through negligence, there is no advantage for beneficiary undertaking.
IV	Is the measure intended to compensate recipient for costs of public service obligation?	If the answer is no, there is advantage for beneficiary undertaking. If the answer is yes and the Altmark conditions hold, there is no advantage for recipient undertaking. If the answer is yes but the Altmark conditions do not hold, the measure constitutes aid which is compatible if the conditions in Art. 86(2) are respected.

2.4 Selectivity: Specific versus general measures

"General" measures of economic policy are not aid. Article 87(1) EC refers to advantages favouring "certain" undertakings or the production of "certain" goods. This has been interpreted over the years to mean that aid must be "selective" or "specific" rather than general. As the CFI ruled in *CETM* case:

"The fact that the aid is not aimed at one or more specific recipients defined in advance, but that is subject to a series of objective criteria pursuant to which it may be granted, within the framework of a predetermined overall budget allocation, to an indefinite number of beneficiaries who are not initially individually identified, cannot suffice to call into question the selective nature of the measure, and, accordingly, its classification as state aid within the meaning of Article 87 (1) of the Treaty. At the very most, that circumstance means that the measure is not an individual aid. It does not, however, preclude that public measure from having to be regarded as a system of aid constituting a selective, and therefore specific, measure if, owing to the criteria governing its application, it procures an advantage for certain undertakings or the production of certain goods, to the exclusion of others."[59]

However, even if it appears that an aid measure procures an advantage for certain undertakings to the exclusion of others, in some rare circumstances it may still escape the Article 87 (1) EC prohibition if it is considered as a general measure. In May 1997, for example, the Commission considered a guarantee scheme aimed at improving the financial structure of SMEs as not constituting aid. The scheme was general (even though it applied only to SMEs) and was self-supporting through the premiums charged to the beneficiary companies.[60]

No concrete definition of "general measures" either in the Commission's practice or the Community Courts' jurisprudence has been given. Some guidance, however, has been given on a case-by-case basis. For instance, measures designed to reduce the taxation of labour for all firms have a relatively greater effect on labour-intensive industries than on capital-intensive industries, without necessarily constituting state aid. Similarly, tax incentives for environmental, R&D or training investment favour only the firms which undertake such investment, but again do not necessarily constitute state aid.[61] Further, measures which apply to persons in accordance with objective criteria without regard to the location, sector or undertaking in which the beneficiary may be employed, are not considered to be state aid.[62]

On the other hand however, general measures which are implemented on a discretionary basis would fall under Article 87(1) EC. A scheme operated

59 Case T-55/99, *Confederación Española de Transporte de Mercancias (CETM) v Commission,* 2000 ECR II-3207, at para. 40.

60 IP/97/438.

61 Commission Notice on the application of the State aid rules to measures relating to direct business taxation, OJ C384, 10/12/1998, at para. 14.

62 Commission Notice on co-operation between national courts and the Commission in the State aid field, OJ C312, 23/11/1995, at para. 7.

by Finland and intended to boost employment by subsidising new jobs was found to be incompatible with the common market because the public authorities had discretion in confirming eligibility and thus in disbursing the subsidies. Hence, for a policy measure to escape Article 87 EC, its application must be general, without any discriminatory effect among undertakings and its benefits must be readily or automatically available to any undertaking.

Measures which appear to be general may still be found to favour certain undertakings or certain goods. For example, a general export credit scheme operated by France in respect of all national products which were exported was found to be aid prohibited by Article 87 EC.[63] The same was found for a scheme of interest rate subsidies on all exports from Greece[64] and for a scheme that exempted all Greek export undertakings from a special single tax on undertakings.[65]

Given the fact that not all undertakings operate under identical conditions, in principle there is no such thing as a general scheme that can apply equally to all undertakings. The Commission and the Court, however, do not attempt to examine the precise ex post effects of a general scheme on company competitiveness. They consider instead whether in principle it applies to all sectors of the economy (i.e. whether it discriminates *a priori* between sectors) and whether any company may, in theory, be eligible to benefit from it.

These indeed are the reasons why, for example, the Commission banned an Italian scheme to promote employment in the footwear industry and a similar French scheme in the textile industry, while it approved a Belgian scheme which also aimed to stimulate employment. The difference between them was that the Belgian scheme, approved in March 1997, reduced the social security contributions of all firms generating new jobs for manual workers in a transparent and objective manner.[66] Previous versions of the same Belgian scheme were rejected by the Commission because they were restricted to certain industries which were exposed to international competition.[67] Nevertheless, the approved scheme does not have the same effect in all sectors of the economy. To the extent that certain sectors employ relatively fewer manual workers (i.e. professional services) or relatively more manual workers (i.e. agriculture) they are bound to enjoy the benefits from the scheme in different proportions.

In summary, the following steps may be followed in determining whether a measure is selective:

---

63 Case C-11/69, *Commission v France,* 1969 ECR 523

64 Case C-57/86, *Greece v Commission,* 1988 ECR 2855

65 Commission Decision 89/659, OJ L394, 30/12/1989.

66 IP/97/251

67 IP/96/1127

Stage	Questions	Outcome
I	Does the measure intend to favour certain firms or class of firms?	If the answer is yes, the measure is selective. If the answer is no, go to Stage II.
II	Is there administrative discretion in its application?	If the answer is yes, the measure is selective. If the answer is no, go to Stage III.
III	Are the results likely to favour in practice certain firms or class of firms?	If the answer is yes, go to Stage IV. If the answer is no, the measure is not selective.
IV	Is the measure open to all firms without any discrimination?	If the answer is yes, the measure is not selective. If the answer is no, the measure is selective.

2.5 Effect on trade and distortion of competition

The conditions under which trade between Member States is affected and competition is distorted for the purposes of Article 87(1) EC are as a general rule inextricably linked. For this reason, if aid is found to have an appreciable effect on trade, it is inevitably found to distort or threaten to distort competition.[68] Confirming its earlier case-law,[69] the ECJ stated in the *Philip Morris v Commission* judgement that when state financial aid strengthens the position of an undertaking compared with other undertakings competing in intra-Community trade, the latter must be regarded as affected by that aid.[70]

2.5.1 Effect on trade

There is no definition or quantitative measure of when aid is capable of affecting trade. It is settled case law however, that aid may affect intra-Community trade even if it is of relatively small amount.[71] Any aid, in turn, is presumed to affect trade unless:

68 Case T-288/97, *Regione Autonoma Friuli Venezia Giulia v Commission,* 2001 ECR II-1169, at paras. 49-50.

69 Case C-173/73, *Commission v Italy* (cited above at No. 22).

70 Case 730/79, *Philip Morris v Commission,* 1980 ECR 2671, at para. 11.

71 Case T-214/95, *Het Vlaamse Gewest v Commission,* 1998 ECR II-717, at para. 48-49 and the case law cited therein.

- It is *de minimis*, or
- Trade is affected only at national level, or
- The situation is wholly outside the EC.

There is no appreciable effect on trade when the total amount of aid over a three-year period does not exceed € 100,000 ("*de minimis*"). This threshold is defined in the Regulation 69/2001 on *de minimis* aid published in January 2001.[72] It is also settled case law that small amounts of aid to an undertaking over a given period do not affect trade between the Member States and are therefore not caught by Article 87(1) EC.[73] The *de minimis* rules do not apply to export aid or aid in the fields of transport, agriculture and fisheries.

In common with other Treaty provisions, Article 87 EC does not cover situations which are purely domestic or completely outside the EU. For example, subsidies granted to hairdressers would not be considered to be aid in the meaning of Article 87 EC because individuals do not normally buy hairdressing services from other Member States.[74] Also, a subsidy to a French company, for example, covering part of the costs of constructing a bridge in Kenya would not normally infringe Article 87 EC, provided of course, that no other EC company would be interested in that project.

However, even if aid is received by an undertaking which sells its products exclusively within the domestic market of a member state, intra-Community trade may still be found to be indirectly affected, if it becomes more difficult for similar products from other Member States to enter that market. A situation of this kind may arise in cases of over-capacity in a particular market, as a result of which domestic production may be maintained or increased, with the end-result that undertakings established in other Member States have less chance of exporting their products to the market in that member state.[75]

Also, aid which is given to an undertaking that exports exclusively to a non-EU country may still have an indirect impact on intra-EU trade, if it displaces exports by companies in other Member States, which are then redirected towards the internal Community market.[76] Similarly, in *AITEC v Commission* the CFI annulled the Commission's decision to approve a general aid scheme on the grounds that the latter should have considered the fore-

---

72 Cited above at No. 9.

73 Case C-351/98, *Spain v Commission*, 2002 ECR I-8031, at para. 51.

74 XXVIth Report on Competition Policy, 1996, at p. 230. The Commission decided to terminate proceedings on aid for firms providing only local passenger transport services in Italy, since the measure was liable to distort competition in that it did not affect trade between Member States.

75 Case 102/87, *France v Commission*, 1988 ECR 4067, at para. 49.

76 Case C-142/87, *Belgium v Commission*, 1990 ECR I-959, at para. 38.

seeable effects of the aid on competition and intra-Community trade.[77]

The Commission is not required to define markets or analyse their structures and the ensuing competitive relationships in order to establish a real effect on trade between Member States, which would anyway be impossible if aid is not yet implemented. If new aid has been granted without prior notification having been given, the Commission is not required to establish whether the aid has a real effect on trade and competition. According to well-established case-law, such a requirement would favour Member States which grant aid in breach of the obligation to notify, to the detriment of those which do notify aid at the planning stage.[78]

2.5.2 Distortion of competition

For aid to be caught under Article 87 EC, it must also be capable of distorting competition. As mentioned above, the conditions under which trade between Member States is affected and competition is distorted are as a general rule inextricably linked. The test defined by the Commission and the Courts for determining the effect on trade and competition is not strict. Small effects on trade are sufficient to conclude on distortion. Similarly, anything that actually disturbs or threatens to disturb the conditions of competition between undertakings from different Member States is sufficient for Article 87(1) EC to apply.

In order to establish whether competition is affected for the purposes of Article 87(1) EC, it is necessary to consider first the definition of the market for the products or services concerned. The market is defined by distinguishing the service or the good in question by virtue of particular characteristics that so differentiate it from other services or other goods that it is only to a small degree interchangeable with those alternatives and affected by competition from them. In that context, the degree of interchangeability between products or services must be assessed in terms of their objective characteristics, as well as the structure of supply and demand on the market, and competitive conditions.[79]

In the *SIDE v Commission* case concerning export aid in the book sector, the CFI criticised the Commission as having committed a manifest error of assessment as regards the definition of the relevant product market. It annulled, thus, the Commission's decision on the grounds that it should have examined the effects of the contested aid on competition and trade between

77 Cases T-447 & 449/93, *AITEC v Commission,* 1995 ECR II-1971, at paras. 139-140.

78 Case T-55/99, *CETM v Commission* (cited above at No. 52, at para. 103 and the case law cited therein).

79 Case T-229/94, *Deutsche Bahn* v *Commission,* 1997 ECR II-1689, at para. 54, and the case-law cited therein.

the other operators carrying on the same activity as that for which the aid was granted, in this case the handling of small orders of French-language books. The Commission, thus, should have defined the market as that of agency export rather than that of the export of French-language books in general.[80]

Competition is distorted, if the aid in question strengthens the competitive position of the recipient, say by reducing its operating or investment costs, in relation to its rivals.[81] Always the relevant question is what would be the competitive position of the recipient in the absence of aid? If this would be worse in relation to its rivals, then aid distorts competition.

Article 87(1) EC is not confined to large amounts of aid, significant distortions of competition or substantial disturbance to trade. Given that Article 87(1) EC requires no quantitative tests, it applies both to direct or indirect effects and actual or potential effects and provided that it focuses on effects rather than the intentions of public policies, it is very difficult for an aid scheme to escape being caught by it, even if it appears to be of a modest amount. It is settled case-law that even aid of a relatively small amount is liable to affect trade between Member States and strengthen the position of the recipient as compared to its competitors.[82]

The argument often advanced by Member States that aid aims to offset alleged competitive disadvantage of the recipient undertakings has never been accepted as such by the Courts or the Commission.

In addition, the fact that a member state seeks to approximate, by unilateral measures, conditions of competition in a particular sector of the economy to those prevailing in other Member States cannot deprive the measures in question of their character as distorting competition. It follows that aid cannot be justified either by the existence of more favourable conditions for undertakings in other Member States or by the competition from those undertakings.[83]

---

80 Case T-155/98, *SIDE v Commission,* 2002 ECR II-1179, at para. 71.

81 Case 234/84, *Belgium v Commission,* 1986 ECR 2263, at para. 22.

82 Case T-214/95, *Vlaams Gewest* v *Commission,* 1998 ECR II-717, at para. 49.

83 Joined cases 6 & 11/69, *Commission v France,* 1969 ECR 523, at para. 20.

CHAPTER II

Exceptions under Article 87 EC

As discussed, Article 87 (1) EC provides that state aid is considered incompatible with the common market and thus prohibited, "save as otherwise provided in this Treaty." In this context, Article 87(2) EC provides that certain aid is automatically compatible with the common market. Secondly, Article 87(3) EC enables the Commission to consider the compatibility of certain aid with the common market on the basis of a number of objectives to be attained. Finally, according to Article 87(3)(e) EC the Council, acting by qualified majority on a proposal from the Commission, may decide in exceptional instances that certain aid may also be considered compatible with the common market.

It is important to state in this context that state aid is in principle considered incompatible with the common market as long as the Member States are not able to give nor has the Commission found any grounds establishing that the aid concerned meets the conditions for exception laid down in Article 87(3) EC.[84]

1. AID THAT IS COMPATIBLE WITH THE COMMON MARKET

The second paragraph of Article 87 EC defines three instances in which state aid is automatically compatible with the common market. In practice, very few cases of aid are authorised every year under Article 87(2) EC. In particular, Article 87(2) EC provides that:

84 Case 730/79, *Philip Morris v Commission,* 1980 ECR 2671, at para. 18.

"2. The following shall be compatible with the common market:

(a) aid having a social character, granted to individual consumers, provided that such aid is granted without discrimination related to the origin of the products concerned;

(b) aid to make good the damage caused by natural disasters or exceptional occurrences;

(c) aid granted to the economy of certain areas of the Federal Republic of Germany affected by the division of Germany, in so far as such aid is required in order to compensate for the economic disadvantages caused by that division."

Aid to individuals must not be linked to their employer. Any such link will be considered as conferring an indirect advantage to certain firms and therefore will have to be examined in the context of the exceptions allowed by Article 87(3) EC. Taken that the basic characteristic of this category is the social character of the aid, the beneficiaries are normally lower income groups, which need financial contribution, such as elderly people, children and handicapped persons.

A particular example is the aviation sector. As the Commission explicitly stated, Article 87(2)(a) EC, which up to now has only rarely been used, may be of certain relevance in the case of direct operational subsidisation of air routes, provided that aid is effectively for the benefit of final consumers. The aid must have a social character, i.e. it must, in principle, only cover specific categories of passengers travelling on a route (e.g. children, handicapped people, low income people). However, in case the route concerned links an underprivileged region, mainly islands, the aid could cover the entire population of this region. The aid has to be granted without discrimination as to the origin of the services, that is to say whatever EEA air carriers operating the services. This also implies the absence of any barrier to entry on the route concerned for all Community air carriers.[85]

The natural disasters or exceptional occurrences for which aid may be given must be out of the ordinary, substantial and unpredictable. Thus, for example, rainfall below normal rates that has a negative effect on agricultural production is not considered to be a natural disaster. By the same token, above normal rainfall that ruins a holiday season is also not considered to be natural disaster for tourist operators. Natural disasters include droughts, tornadoes, forest fires, earthquakes, volcanic eruptions and diseases of plant and animals

---

85 Application of Articles 92 and 93 (now 87 and 88) of the EC Treaty and Article 61 of the EEA agreement to State aids in the aviation sector, OJ C350, 10/12/1994, at section III.3. See also case N 26/2003.

of catastrophic proportions.[86] Also, as has the Commission stated in its guidelines on state aid to agriculture sector, adverse weather conditions such as frost, hail, ice, rain or drought may be assimilated to natural disasters once the level of damage reaches a certain threshold, which has been fixed at 20% of normal production in the less-favoured areas and 30% in other areas.[87] Exceptional occurrences include war, internal disturbances or strikes, and with certain reservations and depending on their extent, major nuclear or industrial accidents and fires which result in widespread loss.

Most notably, during the past couple of years, Article 87(2)(b) EC has been the basis for the authorisation of aid to businesses affected by flooding of rivers and by marine pollution caused by the sinking of oil tankers and to airlines to compensate them for the losses suffered as a result of the closure of US airspace and the increase in insurance premia in the aftermath of the terrorist attacks on New York in September 2001.

Aid in relation to the division in Germany has not been authorised during the past decade.[88] It used to be authorised before German re-unification, when the objective of aid was to offset the effects of the physical division of the country, not the overall effects of the communist economic system in East Germany. In practice, approved aid in the past concerned issues such as extra transport costs, poorer communications, etc.

Needless to mention that the mere fact that state aid is always compatible with the common market in all the above mentioned instances does not exclude Member States from their obligation to notify. Following notification, the Commission decides whether Article 87(2) EC applies to the notified aid or scheme, and only if it does must the Commission rule on the compatibility of the aid in question with the common market.

2. AID THAT MAY BE COMPATIBLE WITH THE COMMON MARKET

Article 87(3) EC defines five instances in which state aid "may be" compatible with the common market. In this regard state aid is not automatically exempted but the Commission has wide discretion to decide on the compatibility of aid scheme with the common market. Responsibility thus for making that determination rests exclusively with the Commission. This is the reason why Article 88 EC and Regulation 659/99 define a procedure whereby Mem-

---

[86] VIIIth Report on Competition Policy, 1978, at p. 164.

[87] OJ C28, 01/02/2000.

[88] See in this respect Joined cases C-57/00 and C-61/00, *Freistaat & Volkswagen v Commission*, 2003 ECR I-9975.

ber States must first notify to the Commission their proposed aid schemes and obtain its authorisation before they implement them. Provided it acts with existing guidelines, the Commission is free to authorise outright, demand changes or reject completely a notified aid scheme. Under Article 88 EC, even if a member state disagrees with the Commission's decision and believes it is mistaken, it should not go ahead with the scheme. It can only challenge that decision before the Court or apply to the Council, if the Commission has not yet completed its investigation. The latter possibility is rarely utilised.

Whenever the Commission examines aid schemes notified by the Member States, it is bound by EC law to authorise only those schemes which fall within the categories defined in Article 87(3) EC. Any other kind of aid must be rejected. This principle is well established in case law by the ruling in the land-mark case involving Dutch aid granted to Philip Morris in the late 1970s.[89]

Article 87(3) EC provides that:

> "3. The following may be considered to be compatible with the common market:
> (a) aid to promote the economic development of areas where the standard of living is abnormally low or where there is serious underemployment;
> (b) aid to promote the execution of an important project of common European interest or to remedy a serious disturbance in the economy of a Member State;
> (c) aid to facilitate the development of certain economic activities or of certain economic areas, where such aid does not adversely affect trading conditions to an extent contrary to the common interest;
> (d) aid to promote culture and heritage conservation where such aid does not affect trading conditions and competition in the Community to an extent that is contrary to the common interest;
> (e) such other categories of aid as may be specified by decision of the Council acting by a qualified majority on a proposal from the Commission."

The categories of aid that are of major interest are the first and the third. The provisions on aid for cultural purposes and aid otherwise defined by the Council are utilised very infrequently. Since the inception of the Community in 1958, the Council has used that provision only twice to define a common framework of subsidies to the shipbuilding industry (replaced European

[89] Case 730/79, *Philip Morris v Commission,* 1980 ECR 2671, at para. 18.

projects by a Commission framework in 2003) and to coal-mining (Regulation 1407/2002).

Article 87(3)(a) EC refers to regional aid and is applicable for regions that are disadvantaged compared to the Community average. According to the Commission guidelines on regional aid,[90] Article 87(3)(a) EC shall apply to regions having a per capita GDP of less than 75% of the Community average. The guidelines further indicate that Article 87(3)(a) EC exemption may normally only be granted for multi-sectoral aid schemes, open in a given region to all firms in the sectors concerned, whereas ad hoc aid to a single undertaking would fall outside the scope of that Article, since it is not regarded as regional aid.[91] However, the Commission does assess ad hoc aid in the context of the guidelines.

Aid under Article 87(3)(b) EC is mostly used to support large research and developments projects with common European interest, such as projects against environmental pollution[92] or projects which aim to strengthen the European electronic industry by creating know-how and research networks throughout Europe in which scientists, producers of components and system-users worked together in order to ensure an independent European position on basic microelectronics technology.[93]

Aid under this Article is also permissible, if it remedies a serious disturbance in the economy of a member state, such as the aid granted to Greece in the context of privatisation of hundreds of Greek firms and public-sector banks as part of a national economic recovery plan. The decisive factor was the particularly serious economic situation in Greece at the time.[94]

Article 87(3)(c) EC covers regional aid and gives Member States the possibility to assist regions which are disadvantaged compared to the national average. The list of regions qualifying for this exemption is decided by the Commission on a proposal by the member state concerned. Aid is also given to facilitate the development of certain economic activities, such as aid for environmental protection, or for the promotion of research, or aid for the rescue and restructuring of firms in difficulty (See Appendices X and VII).

To clarify the kinds of aid that may be compatible with the common market and in order to ensure that its discretion is exercised with proper openness and that the authorities and businesses are clear about their legal position, the Commission has over the years issued a number of notices, communications, guidelines and frameworks which are published in the Official Journal. The

---

90 OJ C74, 10/03/1998, amended by OJ C258, 09/09/2000.

91 Case T-152/99, *HAMSA v Commission,* 2002 ECR II-3049, at paras. 201-209.

92 Case 730/79, *Philip Morris v Commission,* 1980 ECR 2671, at para. 25.

93 XXVth Report on Competition Policy, 1995, at p. 238.

94 XXIst Report on Competition Policy, 1991, at p. 251.

Commission also sends letters to Member States, which are also published eventually. The guidelines for example set out the Commission's views on the meaning of aid for various purposes (e.g. regional development, employment, R&D, rescue and restructuring of companies, etc.), the methods by which aid is calculated, the eligible recipients and the total amount of aid that may be granted. These guidelines, therefore, are indispensable in understanding how the Commission is likely to assess the eligibility or not of a notified aid scheme.

Indeed, the guidelines are intended to assist national, regional and local governments to design aid packages which can be approved by the Commission. This is good practice since there would be considerable waste of public resources if the Commission rejected aid schemes which took months to design simply because the officials responsible were not aware of the criteria that would be used by the Commission to evaluate those schemes.

It should be noted, however, that the legality of these guidelines is a point of contention among legal experts. Since the guidelines are issued by the Commission, they are binding on the latter. The ECJ, has also affirmed that Member States are bound by them if they have agreed to their content.[95] In *Germany v Commission,* the ECJ stated:

> "It should be noted at the outset that, in the exercise of the powers conferred on it by Articles 87 EC and 88 EC, the Commission may adopt guidelines designed to indicate how it intends, under those articles, to exercise its discretion in regard to new aid or in regard to existing systems of aid. When they are based on Article 88(1) EC, those guidelines constitute one element of the regular and periodic cooperation under which the Commission, in conjunction with the Member States, must keep under constant review existing systems of aid and propose to them any appropriate measures required by the progressive development or by the functioning of the common market. In so far as these proposals for appropriate measures are accepted by the a Member State, they are binding on that Member State."[96]

In this respect Article 19 of the Procedural Regulation states that: "Where a Member State concerned accepts the proposed measures and informs the Commission thereof, the Commission shall record that finding and inform the Member State thereof. The Member State shall be bound by its acceptance to implement the appropriate measures."

Therefore, it can be concluded from the above that the wording of Article 19 must be interpreted as also covering guidelines directed to all the Member States.

---

95 Case C-313/90, *CIRFS and Others v Commission,* 1993 ECR I-1125.

96 Case C-242/00, *Germany v Commission,* 2002 ECR I-5603, at paras. 27-28.

3. CRITERIA AND FACTORS IN THE EVALUATION OF STATE AID SCHEMES

The criteria used by the Commission to evaluate aid schemes reveal a clear policy goal: to increase the effect of market forces. Its aim is to control aid so as to eliminate distortions to competition in the internal market. So, even if aid falls within the scope of the exceptions provided by Article 87(3) EC, the Commission will not authorise it if it confers an unnecessary advantage to certain undertakings. For aid to be permitted under Article 87(3) EC, it must seek to remedy some market failure or aim to induce undertakings to do something they would not otherwise do under normal market conditions. Aid must be necessary to offset a certain commercial, structural or regional handicap and must, therefore, be objectively justified.

For example, the Commission approves certain forms and amounts of aid for the promotion of basic scientific research which may not be readily undertaken by private companies, if such research has no immediate commercial applications or if its results cannot be appropriated by the company that undertakes it. The reason for subsidising such research is that the market will under-provide it even if society as whole would gain from it.

3.1 Necessity

The example above suggests that if, in the absence of state aid, undertakings could do on their own what the aid scheme seeks to induce them to do, the Commission would withhold approval of that scheme. Therefore, the first criterion used in the Commission's evaluation of notified aid is whether it is necessary to promote the objectives in Article 87(3)(a) to 87(3)(e) EC.

Most, if not all, cases of notified aid are designed to comply with the various Commission guidelines, frameworks and notices. Once Member States satisfy all the criteria specified in the guidelines etc., they do not need to prove the necessity of aid. That is assumed to hold. For example, the regional guidelines define the areas which suffer from regional handicaps and are, therefore, eligible to receive that kind of aid. Member States do not have to prove further the necessity of aid granted in conformity with those guidelines.

However, some guidelines still require Member States to provide evidence of necessity of aid to induce recipients to do something they would not otherwise do under normal market conditions. This is required by the guidelines on aid for R&D, and for promotion of risk capital.

3.2 Proportionality

The second criterion is whether aid is proportional to the aim it pursues. That is, aid should never exceed the minimum amount necessary to induce recipients to undertake, for example, more research, more investment or hire more people. As most forms of state aid do, irrespective of their objectives, distort competition, proportionality has the important task of trying to achieve a balance between the distortion of competition and the achievement of Community objectives through state aid.

To determine the proportionality of aid, the Commission examines among others the intensity as well as the cumulation of aid.

3.2.1 Aid intensity

Aid intensity is measured as the amount of aid in relation to the costs of production or the costs of investment of the company or project that receives the aid.

If, for example, the cost of an investment in an Article 87(3)(a) EC region is € 500,000 and the company that undertakes the investment receives a subsidy of € 100,000, the gross aid intensity is 20%. This intensity falls below the maximum ceiling of permissible aid for such region, which is fixed by the Regional aid Guidelines at 50%. It is important to note, however, that the Guidelines indicate maximum ceilings. The actual ceiling that applies to each Community region is defined in the Regional Aid Map for each member state that is defined by a Commission decision.

In case of a loan, the Commission calculates the subsidy-equivalent amount. Assume that a government grants a three-year loan of € 3,000,000 at an interest rate of 6% instead of the going market rate of 8%. The loan is to be repaid in linear instalments plus interest, starting at the end of the first year. To determine the aid intensity of this scheme, it is first necessary to measure the amount of subsidy, or grant equivalent, which is included in the subsidised loan.

The subsidy amount for the first year is the principal sum multiplied by the difference in interest rates (2%) and then discounted to the beginning of the year when that aid is given:

i.e. € 3,000,000 x (0.02/1.08) = € 55,557

(The derived amount means that if you pay € 55,557 in a bank (long-term account) at 8% and leave it for a year, at the end of the year it will grow to € 60,000 which is equal to € 3,000,000 x 2%.)

The subsidy for the second year, discounted back to the first year, is:

€ 2,000,000 x $(0.02/1.08)^2$ = € 34,293

The subsidy for the third year is:

€ 1,000,000 x $(0.02/1.08)^3$ = € 15,877

The total amount of the subsidy discounted back to the year it is granted is € 105,725. The total amount of (discounted) interest that the company would have paid at 8% is € 422,903. This means that the aid intensity is just over 25%. Whether this aid intensity is permissible very much depends on where the investment takes place. If it is an Article 87(3)(a) EC region, there is no over-compensation. If, by contrast, it is an Article 87(3)(c) EC region, there is over-compensation as the aid exceeds the standard ceiling of 20%.

If, instead of a subsidised loan, the government in question offered a loan guarantee, there could still be an element of state aid involved. The cash-grant equivalent (CGE) of such aid is the difference between the outstanding loan sum guaranteed, adjusted by the probability of default, and any premium paid by the beneficiary, i.e. CGE = (outstanding sum x risk) – premium. The risk factor is derived from the experience of default on loans in similar circumstances.[97]

In determining the proportionality of aid, the Commission calculates the "extra costs" borne by the recipients of aid. For example, in February 1997 the Commission approved aid scheme for transport in the northern regions of Sweden and allowed the Swedish government to reimburse some of the costs normally borne by businesses for road or rail transport on a scale rising with the distance covered. In the areas with the highest levels of aid, the reimbursement rates ranged from 5% to 45%. The Commission recognised that the northern Scandinavian regions differed from others in the EC because they "suffer specific handicaps in terms of distance and transport costs."[98] A similar scheme was also approved for Finland.[99]

The principle of offsetting regional handicaps has also been re-stated in a case involving aid to Ford (UK) for investment in a factory situated in South Wales. Since that area is eligible for regional assistance (with net grant equivalent, i.e. after tax, ceiling of 20%), the Commission approved in December 1996 a notified aid scheme whose aid intensity was below the aid ceiling for that region. The Commission explained that it was its policy to approve aid in proportion with the regional disadvantages resulting from the investment in the assisted region. It further said that its analysis was based on the tenet that "all areas eligible for regional aid possess a certain minimum degree of net incremental handicaps."[100]

---

[97] For further examples, see the Regional Aid Guidelines (cited above at No. 83, at Annex I).
[98] IP/97/91.
[99] IP/96/1131.
[100] Case N 781/96.

3.2.2 Cumulation of aid

To ensure proportionality, the Commission has devised rules for assessing the "cumulation" of aid from different sources. The various guidelines and frameworks contain the same basic rule on cumulation. No aid from two or more sources may be received for the same underlying costs or expenditure. In the case of regional aid, the two rules on cumulation are: (a) all aid for regional development purposes from all sources (national and Community) must fall below the relevant regional intensity ceilings and (b) the common component of aid for different purposes is subjected to the most favourable intensity ceiling.[101]

The Regional Guidelines mentioned above also require individual notification of large projects even where aid intensity is below the stipulated ceilings. The reason is that large projects have a more pronounced effect on competition so that the Commission adjusts downwards any relevant ceilings. The Multilateral Framework for Large Projects which came into effect on 1 January 2004 requires notification for every case where the amount of gross aid exceeds the allowable amount for investments of € 100 million.

3.3 Operating aid and export aid

The Commission has always taken a very negative position on operating aid. This is defined as aid, which relieves an enterprise of the expenses it would normally have to bear in its day-to-day management or its usual activities. Such aid is not linked to a specific purpose and has no incentive effect on enterprises. It is considered to be very distorting while the distortion is normally not justified by a Community objective. Therefore, operating aid can only exceptionally be authorised. Under current rules, operating aid may be authorised under certain conditions only in Article 87(3)(a) EC regions provided that it is justified in terms of its contribution to regional development and that its level is proportional to the handicaps it seeks to alleviate (e.g. relief of extra transport costs in outermost regions and of environmental taxes).[102]

Operating aid is also exceptionally allowed to relieve ecotaxes and in maritime transport.[103]

---

[101] Commission Communication on the cumulation of regional aid with other aid, OJ C3, 05/01/1985 (no longer in force) and the Regional Aid Guidelines (cited above at No. 83).

[102] Regional Aid Guidelines (cited above at No. 83 at 4.15).

[103] See the guidelines on Environmental aid and on Maritime Transport.

Export aid is already forbidden under the WTO rules and therefore it is not allowed by the EC. An exception is made for certain types of "soft aid", which may very indirectly be linked to export, e.g. aid to participate in international trade.[104]

3.4 Temporary and degressive aid

Eventually, any publicly aided project should be able to survive on its own without continuous assistance from the government. The reason is that government action should not permanently replace normal market mechanisms. Once, for example, a certain market imperfection is corrected, state aid must be withdrawn. The Commission, therefore, examines carefully the duration of aid schemes and considers whether the means by which aid is given are temporary or permanent. Aid given for an indefinite period of time is unlikely to be approved by the Commission. Approvals are normally granted for specific time periods and for the duration of the relevant guidelines in force.

A case in point is the Commission's decision in January 1997 to initiate proceedings against the extension of aid scheme for Sicily. The Commission had approved the renewal for the last time of an earlier scheme in 1994. The scheme provided for loans to manufacturing firms at a reduced rate of interest (4%) in order to finance public contracts that had already been awarded. The scheme itself had been in operation for a total period of eleven years and the difficulties which the Italian government invoked to justify it had persisted during that period. The Commission took the view that the arguments of the Italian government did not justify a further extension because a "solution had to be sought through more general policies."[105] In this case the Italian government claimed that the financial difficulties experienced by the firms in question were caused by the very high cost of bank financing. The Commission was of the opinion that the problem had to be addressed directly by other means rather than by aid to the operation of recipient firms.

In the context of authorising large packages of aid to airlines (e.g. Air France, Iberia, Alitalia, Sabena, Olympic), the Commission has pronounced that in the future it will not authorise aid for industries that have on several occasions in the past received hand-outs from the state. It put forth, therefore, the principle of aid "one time, last time."[106] This principle has been restated

[104] See Commission Regulation (EC) No. 70/2001 on the application of Articles 87 and 88 of the EC Treaty to State aid to small and medium-sized enterprises.
[105] IP/97/36.
[106] XXXth Report on Competition Policy, 2000, at p. 340.

in the recently revised guidelines on aid to rescue and restructuring of firms in difficulty. In practice, "one time, last time" means that the same firm may not receive aid more than once in ten years.

3.5 Conditional approval

Aid falling under Article 87(1) EC, even if it promotes the aims of Article 87(3) EC and is proportional to its objectives, may still distort competition and affect trade in the common market. For this reason, the Commission often attaches particular conditions to its approval of state aid schemes. These conditions seek to minimise the disruption to competition and trade in the internal market and reduce the ability of the assisted company or companies to use the aid they receive for other purposes, such as strengthening their market position in other Member States.

Hence, in the context of restructuring aid the Commission often asks for compensatory actions which relate to measures intended to safeguard competition in the sector where aid is granted. For example, as a condition for approving a very large injection of public capital (FF 20 billion) into Air France, the Commission imposed the condition that Air France would give up certain routes in which it had a dominant position and that a number of its landing slots at Orly airport would be made available to other airlines.[107]

3.6 Promoting international competitiveness

While the Commission is anxious to protect the integrity of the common market, it is equally concerned about the deteriorating competitive position of EC companies in international markets. As a result, it has approved a number of state aid schemes whose aim is to promote European companies and help them compete in international markets. For example, it has authorised Danish and Dutch schemes exempting energy-intensive industries from a carbon dioxide/energy tax introduced in those countries a few years ago.[108]

Aid in the form of tax concessions has been approved for the shipping sectors of EC Member States on the grounds that shipping companies could not otherwise compete in the global markets for maritime transport services. Although the Commission has not imposed any time limitations, it will not allow unlimited amounts of aid for the purpose of improving international

---

[107] Commission Decision 653/94, OJ L254, 31/12/1994.
[108] IP/94/881 and IP/95/1446.

competitiveness. It will still want to know whether aid is necessary and proportional to the aim it pursues.[109]

3.7 Information requirements

A good indication of the factors that the Commission takes into account in its state aid decisions is provided by the questionnaire that Member States answer when notifying proposed aid schemes. This questionnaire has been devised by the Commission and is intended to "dissect" proposed schemes and make them transparent and amenable to quantitative analysis.[110]

The main questions in the questionnaire concern the following:

- agency granting the aid
- aim of aid scheme
- eligible regions or sectors
- eligible costs to be offset by aid (e.g. land, equipment, training, etc.)
- aid instruments (the following are mentioned: direct grant, soft loan, interest subsidy, tax relief, guarantee, other)
- duration of aid
- estimated total amount of aid (e.g. estimated revenue losses due to tax concessions)
- estimated number of recipients
- justification of the compatibility of the scheme with the Treaty.

It is obvious from the above questions that the Commission is unlikely to authorise aid schemes which are not well designed or argued by the Member States.

Finally, it should be well understood that the Commission has considerable discretion in calculating the amount of aid involved in public assistance schemes and in measuring the magnitude of the economic handicap facing the beneficiary companies. Moreover, the discretion is wider in cases involving assessment of complex economic and financial data.[111]

---

[109] Community guidelines on State aid to maritime sector, OJ C13, 17/01/2004.

[110] See the forms attached to Regulation 794/2004. See also the reporting forms attached to the Regional Aid Guidelines and the reporting requirements in the three Regulations of 2001 concerning *de minimis* aid, training aid and aid for SMEs and the 2002 Regulation on employment aid.

[111] Case T-106/95, *FFSA v Commission,* 1997 ECR II-229.

4. OTHER EXCEPTIONS TO ARTICLE 87(1) EC

State aid is in principle considered incompatible with the common market and thus prohibited under Article 87(1) EC, "save as otherwise provided in this Treaty."

There are four possibilities of exceptions in the Treaty. First, Article 36 EC limits the application of the rules on competition to the extent that it is necessary for the operation of the common agricultural policy. In particular, state aid may in certain situations be permitted by the Council for the protection of enterprises handicapped by structural or natural conditions or within the framework of economic development programmes.

Second, Article 73 EC considers as compatible with the Treaty aid which meets the need of coordination of public transport services or represents a reimbursement for the discharge of certain obligations inherent in the concept of public service.

Third, Article 86 EC exempts from the rules of competition, undertakings providing services of general economic interest insofar as compliance with competition rules would prevent them from fulfilling the obligations imposed on them by law. The application of Article 86 EC is reviewed in more detailed later on.

Fourth, Article 87(2)&(3) EC itself allows for certain exceptions, as discussed in the previous section.

4.1 Example: State aid to agriculture

Article 36 EC acknowledges that the common agricultural policy takes precedence over the application of EC competition rules.[112] In determining the extent to which competition rules apply to the production and trade of agricultural products the Council must take account of the objectives set out in Article 33 EC. According to Article 33(1) account must be taken in this respect on increasing agricultural productivity, ensuring a fair standard of living for the agricultural community, stabilising markets, assuring the availability of suppliers and ensuring that suppliers reach consumers at reasonable prices. It is also worth noting that in working out the common agricultural policy and the special methods for its application, account must be taken of the particular nature of agricultural activity, which results from the social structure of agriculture and from structural and natural disparities between the various agri-

---

112 Case C-311/94, *Ijssel Vliet v Minister van Economische Zaken,* 1996 ECR I-5023, at paras. 31-33.

cultural regions, the need to effect the appropriate adjustments by degrees and the fact that in the Member States agriculture constitutes a sector closely linked with the economy as a whole.[113]

In the *ARAP v Commission* case the applicants claimed among others that aid granted by the Portuguese Government in the form of tax relief to DAI, a company operating in the sugar sector, for establishment of a beet sugar refinery plant was contrary to common agricultural policy in the sugar sector, given that it would aggravate Community over-capacity in that sector and would give rise to considerable costs for the intervention scheme.[114] The ECJ pointed towards the need to verify whether the tax relief at issue were compatible with the aims pursued by the Article 33 EC and the rules applicable to sugar production and processing sector. The analysis of those rules showed that the applicants arguments were not such as to call into question the compatibility of the aid concerned.[115]

The particular nature of agricultural activity is furthermore reflected in the secondary Community legislation. While some of the general legal instruments in the State aid field apply to the agricultural sector as well,[116] there is special legislation in place that deals with the specific requirements of the sector: e.g. the new Regulation on the application of Articles 87 and 88 of the EC Treaty to State aid to small and medium sized enterprises active in the production, processing an marketing of agricultural products,[117] which is designed as a block exemption, allows Member States to grant various types of state aid without having to seek the Commission's prior clearance. Furthermore, the Community guidelines for state aid in the agricultural sector[118] which cover most sorts of State aid, such as investment aid, environmental aid, disaster aid, etc. and contain references as to the maximum percentage rates of aid permissible in these fields, to eligible costs and to products for which no aid may be granted.[119] There are Community Guidelines for state aid for advertising (agricultural) products listed in Annex I to the EC-Treaty and certain non-Annex I products[120] and on State aid concerning TSE tests, fallen stock and slaughterhouse waste[121] as well as a Commission communication on Sate

---

[113] Article 33(2) EC.

[114] Case T-82/96, *ARAP v Commission,* 1999 ECR II-1889, at para. 85.

[115] Ibid. at paras. 88-95.

[116] See the Commission website for an overview at: http://europa.eu.int/comm/agriculture/stateaid/leg_en.htm

[117] OJ L1, 03/01/2004

[118] Cited above at No. 80.

[119] E.g. for the manufacture or marketing of products which imitate or substitute for milk and milk products; see Guidelines, at para. 4.2.

[120] OJ C252, 12/09/2001.

[121] OJ C324, 24/12/2002.

aids regarding subsidised short-term loans in agriculture (*crédits de gestion*)[122] and one amending the Community framework on State aid for research and development with a part dedicated to agriculture.[123] See also Annex XI for details regarding the Guidelines and the Regulation on state aid to SMEs involved in the agricultural sector. Finally, the Commission has recently adopted a regulation concerning "*de minimis* aid" for the agriculture and fisheries sectors. According to that regulation, aid of up to € 3000 per farmer and fisherman over a 3 years period is exempted from the notification requirement.[124]

4.2 Example: State aid to transport[125]

The various editions of the state aid scoreboard indicate that about a third of all state aid recorded in the EU is granted to the transport sector and, in particular, to railways.

A recent Commission decision concerning a French aid scheme promoting combined transport provides a good example of how Article 73 EC is interpreted and enforced. The aid is paid to the operators of combined transport services who assemble the various links in the logistical chain. The scheme operated from 2003 to 2007 with an annual budget of some € 30-40 million.

Combined transport is a transport network, which combines road transport with other modes of transport such as inland waterways, rail or shipping. The aid scheme is intended to offset the handicap imposed by the transhipment operations inherent in intermodal chains but absent from door-to-door road transport.

The scheme replaces the operating subsidy per tonne-kilometre which the French state pays to French railways (*Société Nationale des Chemins de Fer* SNCF) and the aid paid by French waterways (*Voies Navigables de France* VNF) to operators who set up scheduled services for the transport of containers by river. It covers all categories of intermodal transport: rail, river and short sea shipping. The aim is to enable combined transport operators to provide competitively priced services in order to promote the development of this transport system. It provides for a flat-rate payment per intermodal transport unit (ITU container) transhipped at a land terminal or port situated on metro-

---

122 OJ C44, 16/02/1996.
123 OJ C48, 13/02/1998.
124 OJ L325, 28/10/2004.
125 See Commission Press Release IP/03/593 of 30 April 2003.

politan French territory and per ITU transiting through a transport hub during national and international land transport for import/export.

This measure is in accordance with the White Paper on European transport policy which the Commission adopted in 2001 and which includes the rebalancing of transport modes in its action programme.

The Commission accordingly decided that the aid was compatible with competition rules. As in the agricultural sector, the special role of transport policy within the EC Treaty is reflected in the State aid regime applicable to the sector as well. Article 73 EC, thus provides an additional basis for permitting State aid granted to rail, road or inland waterway transport operators on the condition that such aid meets the needs of coordination of transport or represents reimbursement for the discharge of certain obligations inherent in the concept of a public service (infra, 4.3.). Secondary legislation such as Council Regulation (EEC) No. 1191/69[126] and Council Regulation (EEC) No. 1107/70[127] contain the details in relation to aid granted to these sectors and to compensation for the discharge of such public services.

The State aid provisions of the EC Treaty apply generally to air transport and maritime transport as well as to the aforementioned sectors insofar as they are not covered by special secondary legislation.[128] The Commission has adopted a favourable approach to certain types of aid in this sector in order to promote or maintain the competitiveness of EC transport operators, e.g. operating aid in the maritime transport sector, with the aim of countering some of the effects of the lower costs in third countries,[129] or certain operating aid for airlines pursuant to Article 87(2)(b) to cover extra insurance and security costs and losses suffered as a consequence of the closure of air space, following the events of September 11, 2001.[130]

---

[126] Regulation (EEC) No. 1191/69 of the Council of 26 June 1969 on action by Member States concerning the obligations inherent in the concept of a public service in transport by rail, road and inland waterway, OJ L156, 28/06/1969, as amended by Council Regulation (EC) No. 1893/91 of 20 June 1991 amending Regulation (EEC) No. 1191/69 on action by Member States concerning the obligations inherent in the concept of a public service in transport by rail, road and inland waterway, OJ L169, 29/06/1991.

[127] Regulation (EEC) No. 1107/70 of the Council of 4 June 1970 on the granting of aids for transport by rail, road and inland waterway OJ L130, 15/06/1970.

[128] See in this respect the new Community guidelines on state aid to maritime transport, OJ C13, 17/01/2004.

[129] Connor Quigley and Anthony M. Collins, "*EC State Aid Law and Policy*", 2003, at p. 232.

[130] XXXI Report on Competition Policy, 2001, at para. 446.

4.3 Services of general economic interest (SGEI)

The status of services of SGEI under the rules of competition is being considered at the highest political level in the EC. For this reason it is worth exploring in some detail the policy of the Commission and the views of the Community Courts on state aid to providers of SGEI. As mentioned earlier, a scheme that is found to be state aid within the meaning of Article 87(1) EC may be exempted under the provisions of Article 86(2) EC. The exception of Article 86(2) EC applies only to providers of SGEI.

The Treaty does not define SGEI. SGEI fall within the scope of EC competition rules precisely because they are economic in nature. Member States are free to designate services as being in the general economic interest and this designation may vary among the Member States. Member States have the right to turn into economic certain services, which may not be economic in other Member States (e.g. provision of supplementary pensions). However, the ECJ has identified certain characteristics that justify a service to be regarded as being in the general economic interest. Such services:

- must be important to consumers,
- must be open to all consumers,
- must be provided at uniform terms and predetermined quantity, price and regularity.[131]

Where providers of SGEI cannot generate sufficient revenue, public authorities may grant them state aid. This kind of aid may, under certain conditions, be compatible on the basis of the second paragraph of Article 86 EC. The application of Article 86(2) EC is conditional on the member state defining the content of the obligations and duties imposed in entrusting the particular task, and on these obligations being specific to the particular undertaking and its business, being linked to the subject-matter of the SGEI in question and being designed to make a direct contribution to satisfying that interest.[132]

More specifically, the exception in Article 86(2) EC applies only when restrictions to competition are necessary and proportional to the intended result. Two conditions need to be satisfied in order to prove necessity and proportionality:

(1) The execution of the tasks of SGEI cannot be carried out without restricting competition; this also means that there is no alternative, less restrictive, option for the designated operator to supply the market.

---

[131] Case C-393/92, *Municipality of Almelo and others v NV Energiebedrijf Ijsslmij,* 1994 ECR I-1477, at para. 48.

[132] Case C-159/94, *France v Commission,* 1997 ECR I-5815, at para. 68.

(2) The restriction is the minimum or smallest possible.

In addition, the Commission checks whether a third condition is satisfied, namely, that the restriction is not contrary to the common European interest by obstructing intra-Community trade to an unwarranted degree.

Much of the case law that has clarified how Article 86(2) EC may be enforced refers to utilities such as telecommunications, postal services, electricity distribution, etc. In this connection, the ECJ has acknowledged that the exception of Article 86(2) EC may be invoked for the purpose of maintaining the "economic equilibrium" of the undertakings entrusted with the supply of SGEI.[133]

Since under Article 87 EC a state measure must be judged on the basis of its effects on competition, the question that arises is whether a provider of SGEI, who incurs higher costs than otherwise, may be compensated by the public authority that imposes the SGEI obligation. In one of its earliest pronouncements on the issue of compensation of providers of SGEI, the ECJ veered away from examining compensation in terms of its effects. In a ruling handed down in 1985 in a case concerning the extra costs generated by the obligation imposed by France on certain undertakings to dispose of waste oils, the ECJ stated that those:

> "indemnities do not constitute aid within the meaning of Articles 87 EC, but rather consideration for the services performed by the collection or disposal undertakings."[134]

Public authorities in France paid to the collecting companies indemnities not exceeding their actual annual costs as a form of compensation.

In line with the *ADBHU* ruling, the Commission held for a long time the view that financial benefits granted by Member States to compensate for the additional burden of extra public service duties do not constitute state aid. For example, in the Community guidelines on state aid to maritime transport,[135] it is stated that "the Commission's practice in assessing contracts relating to PSOs (public service obligations) is generally to consider that reimbursement of operating losses incurred as a direct result of fulfilling certain public service obligations is not state aid within the meaning of Article 87(1) of the Treaty."

---

[133] Case C-320/91, *Paul Corbeau,* 1993 ECR I-2533, at para. 21. See also *Municipality of Almelo and others v NV Energiebedrijf Ijsslmij* (cited above at No. 124, at para. 49).

[134] Case 240/83, *Procureur de la République v ADBHU,* 1985 ECR 531, at para. 18.

[135] OJ C20, 05/07/1997.

The Commission's practice has been contradicted by recent rulings of the CFI, starting with the judgement in *FFSA*, which concerned a Commission decision that certain tax concessions granted to the French postal service in order to offset its public service obligations were not state aid. In that decision the CFI took the opposite approach to the Commission and concluded that the measures in question did constitute state aid, even though they could be deemed compatible with the common market under Article 86(2) EC.[136]

Then, the ECJ presented its judgement in the *Ferring* case and reversed the case law generated by the CFI and which until that moment held that compensation for extra costs was state aid. That case concerned the preferential tax treatment of wholesale distributors of medicines in France. France argued that the preferential tax treatment in the form of tax exemptions was justified on the grounds that public service obligations imposed extra costs on the wholesalers. State aid compensated them for being obliged to deliver medicines within 24 hours of receiving a request and for maintaining a full range of stocks.

The ECJ upheld the above argument stating that a tax advantage enjoyed by undertakings entrusted with the operation of a public service did not constitute an economic advantage and could not, thus, be interpreted as state aid, in so far as that advantage did not exceed the additional costs of performing the public service. The reason being that the recipients would obtain no advantage over competitors for as long as the aid received from the state would not exceed the amount of those extra costs.[137]

The above question was also an issue at point in the recent ECJ's rulings in *Altmark* and *Chronopost.*[138] The principle enunciated in *Ferring* has been confirmed and elaborated by the ECJ in *Altmark.* The ECJ laid down four conditions in order for compensation for public service obligation not to constitute state aid:

> "First, the recipient undertaking must actually have public service obligations to discharge, and the obligations must be clearly defined.
> Second, the parameters on the basis of which the compensation is calculated must be established in advance in an objective and transparent manner.

---

[136] Case T-106/95, *FFSA v Commission*, 1997 ECR II-229, at para. 178; upheld on appeal at Case C-174/97P, *FFSA v Commission*, 1998 ECR I-1303.

[137] Case C-53/00, *Ferring SA v Agence centrale des organismes de securite sociale,* 2001 ECR I-9067, at para. 33.

[138] Case C-280/00, *Altmark Trans,* 2003 ECR I-7747 and Joined Appeal Cases C-83/01 P, C-93/01 P and C-94/01 P *Chronopost v Ufex and Others,* 2003 ECR I-6993. See also the earlier ruling of the CFI Case T-613/97 *Ufex and Others v Commission,* 2000 ECR II-4055 and Joined Cases C-34/01 to 38/01, *Enirisorse Spa*, 2003, not yet reported.

Third, the compensation cannot exceed what is necessary to cover all or part of the costs incurred in the discharge of public service obligations, taking into account the relevant receipts and a reasonable profit for discharging those obligations.
Fourth, where the undertaking which is to discharge public service obligations is not chosen pursuant to a public procurement procedure which would allow for the selection of the tenderer capable of providing those services at the least cost to the community, the level of compensation needed must be determined on the basis of an analysis of the costs which a typical undertaking, well run and adequately provided with means of transport so as to be able to meet the necessary public service requirements, would have incurred in discharging those obligations, taking into account the relevant receipts and a reasonable profit for discharging the obligations."[139]

In the *Chronopost* judgement the ECJ went further to limit the scope of the above *Almark* fourth condition. The ECJ annulled the decision of the CFI, which had also put aside the previous Commission decision,[140] insofar as it found that the logistical and commercial assistance provided by La Poste, the French postal administration, to its affiliate company SFMI-Chronoposte, which is active in the market of express courier services, constituted state aid within the meaning of Article 87(1) EC. The CFI in reaching its decision indicated that the remuneration received by La Poste in return for the provision of logistical and commercial assistance, was not sufficient to exclude any aid element, as La Poste, by virtue of its position as the sole public undertaking operating in a reserved sector had been able to provide that assistance at lower costs that a private operator not enjoying the same rights would have been able to do so. It went also further to stress that the Commission should at least have checked that the payment received in return by La Poste was comparable to that demanded by a private holding company or a private group of undertakings not operating in a reserved sector, pursuing a structural policy, whether general or sectorial – and guided by long-term prospects.[141]

The ECJ took the view that the CFI erred in making the above assessment without taking into account the fact that an undertaking such as La Poste was in a situation very different from that of a private undertaking acting under normal market conditions. La Poste was at the time operating in a market network with substantial infrastructures and resources, which would never had

139 Ibid., at paras 88-93.
140 *SFMI-Chronopost*, Commission Decision 98/365, OJ L164, 09/06/1998.
141 Case T-613/97, *Ufex and Others v Commission* (cited above at No. 131, at paras. 74-75).

been created by a private undertaking. As a result, in the absence of any possibility of comparing the situation with that of a private group of undertakings not operating in a reserved sector, the ECJ put aside the judgement of the CFI and upheld the Commission's decision excluding the existence of state aid in the provision of logistical and commercial assistance by La Poste to Chronopost.[142]

Following the recent case law, where public service compensation (PSC) is held not to constitute state aid within the meaning of Article 87(1) EC, if certain conditions are met, the Commission has now come with three draft new measures (published in its website on 27 February and 1 March 2004) to clarify the conditions under which a public service compensation can be compatible with the common market in accordance with Article 86 (2) EC: a Commission directive amending Directive 80/723 on the transparency of financial relations between MS and public undertakings; a Commission Decision on the application of Article 86 EC to state aid that compensates for public service obligations; and a Community Framework for state aid in the form of public service compensation.

The Decision applies to all undertakings in all sectors that have an annual turnover less than (…) [not yet decided] and to hospitals and social housing undertakings, with the condition that they provide SGEI. In so far as it constitutes state aid, PSC is compatible with the common market and need not be notified provided that the public service obligations are precisely defined and officially assigned and the PSC should not exceed the costs of the public service obligations, taking into account revenues and reasonable profit. Profit must not normally exceed the average rate in the sector concerned and must be adjusted to the risk incurred by the undertakings by virtue of the intervention of the Member State.

The Framework applies to all sectors except transport and public service broadcasting. According to the Framework, where the criteria laid down in *Altmark* are not met, PSC may be compatible pursuant to Article 86 (2) EC, if the SGEI are clearly and officially assigned, the PSC does not exceed the costs of the public service obligations, taking into account revenues and reasonable profit, the method of calculation is specified and recoupment of overcompensation is possible.

---

[142] Joined cases C-83/01, C 93/01 and C-94/01 P, *Chronopost v Ufex and Others* (cited above at No. 49, at paras. 35-41).

CHAPTER III

State Aid Procedures

1. TREATY PROVISIONS

The rules on state aid procedures are laid down in Article 88 EC, according to which the Commission has the sole responsibility to supervise the plans of Member States to grant or alter aid and to keep under constant review all systems of aid existing in those Member States.

Article 88 EC reads:

"1. The Commission shall in cooperation with Member States, keep under constant review all systems of aid existing in those states. It shall propose to the latter any appropriate measures required by the progressive development or by the functioning of the common market.

2. If, after giving notice to the parties concerned to submit their comments, the Commission finds that aid granted by a state or through state resources is not compatible with the common market having regard to Article 87, or that such aid is being misused, it shall decide that the state concerned shall abolish or alter such aid within a period of time to be determined by the Commission.

If the state concerned does not comply with this decision within the prescribed time, the Commission or any other interested state may, in derogation from the provisions of Articles 226 and 227, refer the matter to the Court of Justice direct.

On application by a Member State, the Council may, acting unanimously, decide that aid which that state is granting or intends to grant shall be considered to be compatible with the common market, in derogation from the provisions of Article 87 or from the regulations provided for in Article 89, if such a decision is justified by exceptional circumstances. If, as regards the aid in question, the Commission has already initiated the procedure provided for in the first subparagraph of this paragraph, the fact that the state concerned has made its application to the Council shall have the effect of suspending that procedure until the Council has made its attitude known.

If, however, the Council has not made its attitude known within three months of the said application being made, the Commission shall give its decision on the case.

3. The Commission shall be informed, in sufficient time to enable it to submit its comments, of any plans to grant or alter aid. If it considers that any such plan is not compatible with the common market, having regard to Article 87, it shall without delay initiate the procedure provided for in paragraph 2. The Member State concerned shall not put its proposed measures into effect until this procedure has resulted in a final decision."

In order to increase transparency and legal certainty, Council Regulation 659/1999 of 22 March 1999 was adopted (hereinafter the "Procedural Regulation"), which lays down detailed rules for the application of Article 88 EC.[143] Therefore, Article 88 EC and the Procedural Regulation must be read together.

Finally, the Community Courts' jurisprudence has developed and established a consistent practice for the application of Article 88 EC, as the sections below reveal.

2. COMMISSION'S SUPERVISORY CONTROL

2.1 Introduction

The Community's system of control of state aid requires Member States to notify their aid schemes to the Commission and obtain its authorisation before they implement them. Article 88 EC is clear in this respect. Member states must wait for the final decision of the Commission before they implement a

[143] OJ L83, 27/03/1999. A new Commission Regulation 794/2004 (hereinafter the 'Implementing Regulation') has been adopted to facilitate among others the preparation by Member States of state aid notifications (cited above at No. 12).

new scheme or even modify an existing one. Otherwise they risk being brought before the Community Courts.

The Commission's discretion and power is considerable. Although the Treaty provides for the possibility of Member States to petition the Council on the basis of Article 88(2) EC and ask it to decide on national state aid schemes on the basis of unanimity, this is an option which is used rarely and mostly in relation to agricultural products.[144] In practice such decisions are the sole responsibility of the Commission. Not only is the Commission entrusted with vetting of aid schemes, it may also order suspension of aid given without authorisation, even if it would have been authorised, had it been notified. Moreover, the Commission may order the suspension of legally provided aid until illegal aid is recovered in cases were aid would be cumulated and exceed allowable ceilings.

During a typical year the Commission examines about 400 to 500 schemes. This number has declined by about 130-140 cases since early 2001 as a result of the "block exemptions" coming into force. Regulations exist on aid to SMEs, training and employment, which do not require notification if the aid fully complies with their provisions, as is discussed below.

The Commission's supervision includes two procedural steps: the preliminary examination of the notification and the formal investigation procedure. These procedural steps apply in a different manner for each one of the different categories of aid (i.e. new aid, unlawful aid, misuse of aid and finally existing aid). Before, however, proceeding into an analysis of each one of them, it is worth pointing out the differences between new and existing aid as well as between individual aid and aid schemes.

---

[144] An instance of use of Article 88(2) was when the Council, on 21 January 2002, following an application from the Portuguese Government, declared compatible with the common market a grant of aid by Portugal to the pig farmers in order to help them repaying an original aid, which was granted to the beneficiaries before the Commission decided as to its compatibility with the common market. That original aid was eventually declared incompatible and was ordered to be repaid. The case came before the ECJ (Case C-110/02, *Commission v Council*), where the Commission asked for the annulment of the Council's decision. A.G. Jacobs in his opinion delivered on 11 December 2003 states that Article 88(2) does not entitle the Council to adopt decisions in respect of aid which has previously been the subject of a negative Commission decision. The contrary would certainly jeopardise the effective and impartial control of State Aid and would clearly set at nought the allocation of responsibility envisaged by the Treaty. The Court adopted this option and found in favour of the Commission

2.2 New aid versus existing aid

The notions of new and existing aid are given in Article 1 of the Procedural Regulation. New aid means all aid, which is not existing. Falling into this category are new aid schemes, individual aid that is not awarded on the basis of a notified aid scheme, individual aid that is awarded on the basis of a notified scheme and any alterations to existing aid.[145]

Existing aid (aid schemes and individual aid) is aid that used to be in operation before the establishment of the Community or before a member acceded to the Community or the Union.[146] Falling into the category of existing aid is also aid that is implemented after approval by the Commission or by the Council; aid that was notified to the Commission and the latter has not taken a decision within the required two-month period; aid that was held to be unlawful but the ten year limitation period for recovery has expired; and aid which is deemed to be an existing aid because it can be established that at the time it was put into effect it did not constitute aid, and subsequently became aid due to the evolution of the common market and has not in the meantime been altered by the Member State.[147] Finally, new aid that has been notified and approved by the Commission becomes existing aid.

In a landmark case the ECJ ruled that unless the Commission challenges an existing aid scheme (or the Member States object to it at the time of the accession negotiations), the new Member may continue to operate it without having any legal obligation, like existing Member States, to obtain prior approval from the Commission. However, the Member State concerned needs the Commission's approval for any additions or modifications to an existing scheme, which are made after it joins the EU. In particular, the ECJ has declared that:

> "(e)xisting aid may be implemented as long as the Commission has not found it to be incompatible with the common market."[148]

2.3 Individual aid versus aid scheme

New or existing aid can be either individual aid or aid scheme. According to Article 1(e) of the Procedural Regulation, individual aid shall mean aid that is

[145] According to Article 4(1) of the Implementing Regulation, an alteration to existing aid is any change, other than modifications of a purely formal or administrative nature as these cannot affect the evaluation of the compatibility of the aid measure with the common market. An increase in the original budget of an existing aid by up to 20% is not considered an alteration to existing aid.

not awarded on the basis of aid scheme and notifiable awards of aid on the basis of aid scheme. On the other hand, paragraph 1(d) of the Procedural Regulation refers to aid scheme as meaning any act on the basis of which, without further implementing measures being required, individual aid awards may be made to undertakings defined within the act in a general and abstract manner, and any act on the basis of which, aid, which is not linked to a specific project, may be awarded to one or several undertakings.

The difference between individual aid and aid scheme lies in the notification procedure requirements. Thus, in the case of aid scheme, only the scheme has to be notified and not the individual aid awards included therein, whereas in regard to individual aid, it always needs to be notified. Besides, the Commission's approval of aid scheme is without prejudice to compliance with industry-specific aid rules. For example all aid, which the public authorities plan to grant to an individual project or an overall project under authorized aid schemes for a firm or firms operating in the motor vehicle industry must be notified before being granted if, for aid amounts exceeding € 5 million, the aid intensity exceeds 30% of the corresponding regional aid ceiling.[149]

---

[146] By way of derogation to the previous general rule that pre-treaty or pre-accession aid is existing aid, the 1994 Act of Accession already drew the necessary consequences from the fact that, already in 1994, prior to their accession in 1995, Austria, Finland and Sweden, had been subject to state aid obligations under the EEA Agreement. Likewise, for the last accession, Annex IV, chapter 3, paragraph 1, to the 2003 Act of Accession also does not automatically grant "existing aid" status. On the other hand, it provides for three different types of measures, which were put into effect before accession and are still applicable after that date, which are regarded as existing aid.

- The first on covers aid measures put into effect in a new Member State before 10 December 1994.
- The second one consists of a list of state aid measures attached to the Accession Treaty. A list of 223 existing measures was attached therein. These could be submitted until the end of September 2002.
- The third type of existing aid covers other measures submitted to the Commission, which were assessed by the state aid monitoring authority prior to accession and found to be compatible with the *acquis* and to which the Commission did not raise an objection, the so-called "Interim mechanism".

All measures still applicable after the date of accession, which constitute state aid and which do not fall under one of the previous categories shall be considered as new aid upon accession. This mechanism does not apply to agriculture and transport sectors, given that both work with a positive list of aid measures, which were put into effect before accession and are still applicable thereafter. These measures are considered as existing aid for a period of three years. Thus, they need to be submitted within a certain period after accession. Fisheries sector on the other hand, follows the general regime.

3. NOTIFICATION OF AID

3.1 Basic principles

According to Article 2(1) of the Procedural Regulation, any plans to grant new aid shall be notified to the Commission in sufficient time by the Member State concerned. Member States may notify their plans even if they consider that Article 87(1) EC does not come into play, as long as there is some reason to suspect that aid may be involved. Although, the Procedural Regulation, does not explicitly state that non-aid plans should be notified, it indicates in Article 4(2) that the Commission shall issue a decision in any case it finds that the notified measure does not constitute aid.

As mentioned above, and according to Article 3 of the Procedural Regulation, aid notifiable shall not be put into effect before the Commission has taken, or is deemed to have taken, a decision authorising such aid. The question that arises in this context is when aid is put into effect? It is not necessary that aid needs to be paid in order to be considered as being put into effect. "Putting into effect" is taken to mean also the conferment of powers enabling the aid to be granted without further formality (e.g. aid is put into effect and implemented as long as a legislative framework to grant the aid in question has been adopted). In this respect, the Commission has recommended that Member State authorities write a reserve clause into legislation whereby the aid-granting body can make payments only after the Commission has cleared

---

[147] See Joined Cases T-195/01 and T 207/01, *Government of Gibraltar v Commission,* 2002 ECR II-2309, at para. 121, where the CFI held that for a specific measure to be defined as new or existing aid pursuant to Article 1(b)(v) of the Procedural Regulation, this must be determined independently of any previous Commission administrative practice. Article 1(v) of the Procedural Regulation also states that where certain measures become aid following the liberalisation of an activity by Community law, such measures shall not be considered as existing aid after the date fixed for liberalisation. This, however, goes against a ruling of the CFI in the *Alzetto Mauro* case (this decision however was given before the adoption of the Procedural Regulation), where the CFI stated that "a system of aid that already existed in a certain market that was initially closed to competition before its liberalisation (was) also to be regarded as existing aid in the time from the liberalisation." (see joined cases T-298/97, 312/97, 313/97, 315/97, 600-607/97, 1/98, 3-6/98, 23/98, *Alzetto Mauro and Others v Commission,* 2000 ECR II-2319). It is still to be seen how case law will be developed in this instance.

[148] Case C-387/92, *Banco Exterior de España v Ayuntamiento de Valencia*, 1994 ECR I-877, at para. 20. (cited above at no. 51, at para. 20).

[149] Commission communication on the modification of the Multisectoral Framework on regional aid for large investment projects (2002) with regard to the establishment of a list of sectors facing structural problems and on a proposal of appropriate measures pursuant to Article 88 paragraph 1 of the EC Treaty, concerning the motor vehicle sector and the synthetic fibres sector, OJ C263, 01/11/2003.

the aid.[150]

However, there are a number of exceptions from the notification requirement. Firstly, notification is not required in case of *de minimis* aid. According to Article 2 of Commission Regulation No. 69/2001 on the application of Articles 87 and 88 of the EC Treaty to *de minimis* aid,[151] aid measures shall not fall under the notification requirement of Article 88(3) EC if the total amount of aid granted to any one enterprise does not exceed € 100,000 over any period of three years. Secondly, notification is not required for aid measures covered by an authorised aid scheme. In that case, the Commission shall examine whether the aid measure is covered by the authorised aid scheme decision and satisfies thus the conditions set therein. For this purpose, it must ask Member States to supply it with all necessary information. Only after having concluded this procedural step can the Commission, assess the compatibility of the aid measure.[152] Finally, aid covered by group exemption regulations does not need to be notified. According to Article 1(1) of Council Regulation 994/98 on the application of Articles 92 (now 87) and 93 (now 88) of the Treaty establishing the European Community to certain categories of horizontal aid, the Commission may declare that aid in favour of small and medium-sized enterprise (SMEs), research and development, environmental protection, employment and training and certain regional aid shall be compatible with the common market and shall not be subject to the notification requirements of Article 88(3) EC.[153]

In the case of aid measures, which satisfy all the conditions laid down in the above Regulations, Member States are instead required to submit to the Commission a summary description of the aid measure within 20 working days following the implementation of the measure. This summary information is published in the Official Journal. Where the aid measure satisfies all the conditions laid down in the *de minimis* Regulation, there is not even a requirement to submit such summary information.

---

[150] XXIIIrd Report on Competition Policy 1993, at p. 250

[151] Cited above at No. 72.

[152] Case C-47/91, *Italy v Commission*, 1994 ECR I-4635, at paras 33-35, the so-called "Italgrani injunction".

[153] OJ L142, 14/05/1998. Pursuant to this power, the following Regulations were adopted: Commission Regulation (EC) No 68/2001 of 12 January 2001 on the application of Article 87 and 88 of the EC Treaty to training aid, OJ L10, 13/01/2001, Commission Regulation (EC) No 69/2001 of 12 January 2001 on the application of Article 87 and 88 of the EC Treaty to *de minimis* aid (cited above at No. 72), Commission Regulation (EC) No 70/2001 of 12 January 2001 on the application of Article 87 and 88 of the EC Treaty to State aid to small and medium-sized enterprises, OJ L10, 13/01/2001, Commission Regulation (EC) No 2204/2002 of 12 December 2002 on the application of Article 87 and 88 of the EC Treaty to State aid for employment, OJ L337, 13/12/2002.

It is worth noting that the 2001 and 2002 block exemption Regulations require in addition that Member States maintain records of all aid they grant over a ten-year period pursuant to those Regulations and that they submit annual reports to the Commission.

3.2 Completeness of notification

According to Article 2(2) of the Procedural Regulation, in a notification, the Member States shall provide all necessary information, in order to enable the Commission to decide on the compatibility or incompatibility of the aid with the common market. The notification must be complete for the purposes of both the preliminary examination and the formal investigation procedure, as provided for in Article 4(5) and 5 of the Procedural Regulation.[154] Also, as Article 27 of the Procedural Regulation provides, the Commission is empowered to adopt implementing provisions concerning the form, content and other details of notifications. Pursuant to the powers conferred by Article 27, the Commission has recently adopted new procedural rules,[155] including standard notification forms to be used by Member States for the notification pursuant to Article 88(3) EC Treaty of new aid schemes and individual aid in all categories of aid. For reasons of legal certainty, the Commission urges the Member States to use these forms even when a non-aid measure is notified.

Where the Commission considers that the information provided by the Member State concerned is incomplete, it shall request all necessary additional information within a prescribed period (Article 5(1) of Procedural Regulation). If the Member State does not provide the information requested within that period or provides incomplete information, the Commission shall send a reminder, allowing an additional period within which the information shall be provided (Article 5(2)). The notification will be considered as complete, if within two months from its receipt, or from the receipt of any additional information requested, the Commission does not request any further information. Needless to mention that, the period of two months, within which the Commission has to take a decision following a preliminary examination, shall begin on the day following the receipt of a complete notification (Article 4(5)).

According to Article 5(3) of the Procedural Regulation, the notification

---

[154] It should be stated in this respect that the ECJ has taken the view that, for the purposes of the preliminary investigation, it was sufficient for a notification to contain such information as would enable it to form a *prima facie* opinion of the compatibility of the aid with the common market (Case C-99/98, *Austria v Commission*, 2001 ECR I-1101, at para. 53).

[155] Cited above at No. 12.

shall be deemed to be withdrawn, if the requested information is not provided within the prescribed period, unless before the expiry of that period, either the period has been extended with the consent of both the Commission and the Member State concerned, or the latter, in a duly reasoned statement, informs the Commission that it considers the notification to be complete because the additional information requested is not available or has already been provided.

3.3 Preliminary examination procedure

Member States concerned should, pursuant to Article 2(1) of the Procedural Regulation and Article 88(3) EC, notify to the Commission in sufficient time any plans to grant new aid, in order to enable it to submit its comments. The Commission shall examine the notification as soon as it is received (Article 4(1)) and has a two-month time-limit to issue a decision. This period shall begin on the day following the receipt of a complete notification (Article 4(5)). The preliminary examination may also be initiated on a complaint by a competitor or *ex officio*. In that case, however, the two-month period does not apply, but the Commission shall examine all information in its possession without delay and request, if necessary, the Member State concerned for additional information (Article 10(1) and (2) of Procedural Regulation).[156]

During this preliminary stage the Commission has sufficient time for reflection and investigation so that it can form a *prima facie* opinion on the notified aid plans, thus enabling it either to conclude, without the need for detailed examination, that the aid is compatible with the common market or, by contrast, to make a finding that the content of those plans raises doubts as to their compatibility.

In that respect, as ruled in the *Portugal v Commission* case:

> "(...) the Commission is required to examine all the facts and points of law brought to its notice by persons, undertakings and associations whose interests may be affected by the granting of the aid. It is therefore in the light of both the information notified by the state concerned and that provided by any complainants that the institution must make its assessment in the context of the preliminary examination (...)."[157]

---

[156] See Order of the CFI of 27 November 2002 in Case T-291/01, *Dessauer Versogungs- und Verkehrsgesellschaft and Others v Commission* (2002 ECR II-5033), where the CFI stated that "the actual period of 10 months which the Commission took to adopt the Decision (on a complaint raised by the applicants) does not enable it to be said that the Decision was not taken, in the circumstances of this case, within a reasonable period" (at para. 16).

Following the conclusion of the preliminary examination, the Commission may either decide that the notified measure does not constitute aid, possibly because it does not satisfy the conditions of Article 87(1) EC (Article 4(2) of the Procedural Regulation), or it may decide not to raise objections and declare, thus, the notified measure as compatible with the common market, specifying the exception applied under the Treaty (Article 4(3)), or finally that there are doubts as to the compatibility of the measure with the common market, on the basis of which the Commission shall initiate proceedings, pursuant to Article 88(2) EC (Article 4(4)).

When the Commission does not take any of the above decisions within the prescribed two-month period, the notified aid shall be deemed to have been authorised by the Commission (Article 4(6) of the Procedural Regulation). The Member State concerned may thereupon implement the measures in question after giving the Commission prior notice thereof, unless the Commission decides to initiate formal proceedings within a period of 15 working days following receipt of the notice to implement the measure.[158]

3.4 Formal investigation procedure

3.4.1 Initiation of proceedings

Whenever the Commission finds, as the result of the preliminary investigation procedure, that there are doubts as to the compatibility of the notified aid plan with the common market, it shall open the formal investigation procedure, having regard to Article 88(2) EC and Article 4(4) of the Procedural Regulation. The Member State concerned is informed of the initiation of proceedings by letter, whereas the other Member States and interested third parties are informed by a notice published in the OJ, pursuant to Article 26(2) of the Procedural Regulation.

The Commission is obliged to open the formal investigation procedure whenever it has serious difficulty in determining the compatibility of aid with

---

[157] Case C-204/97, *Portugal v Commission,* 2001 ECR I-3175, at para. 35.

[158] As regards prior notice under Article 4(6) of the Procedural Regulation, the Court in *Spain v Commission* has stated the provisions do not require any particular procedural formality. It went on by stating: "Unlike the initial step of notifying new aid, receipt of which must, under Article 1 of the (Procedural) Regulation, be acknowledged by the Commission to the Member State in question, prior notice of implementation is not subject to any requirements beyond those relating to the various stages of the pre-litigation procedure before the Commission. In a footnote to Annex I to its Guide to procedures in State Aid Cases, the Commission has expressly accepted that time-limits for the various kinds of action are 'started by the receipt of correspondence (…) or dispatch if the correspondence is faxed" (Case C-398/00, *Spain v Commission,* 2002 ECR I-5643, at para. 23).

the common market.[159] The opening of formal investigation is also likely in cases where the time of the preliminary investigation procedure exceeded the prescribed two-month period.[160] It must be pointed out that, in accordance with the purpose of Article 88(3) of the Treaty and the Commission's duty of good administration, the Commission may, in the context of the preliminary procedure, find it necessary to request supplementary information from a notifying Member State. Whilst such requests are not proof of the existence of serious difficulties, they may, in conjunction with the duration of the preliminary examination, be evidence thereof. As the CFI has stated:

> "A Member State that gives the Commission incomplete notification, under Article 93(3) of the Treaty (now Article 88(3) EC), of a plan to grant aid and is then reluctant to provide information which would assist the Commission, despite repeated requests on the latter's part, is responsible for prolonging the examination procedure. Such an extension of the examination procedure can, by its very nature, indicate the existence of serious difficulties and the Commission is not entitled to rely on the fact that the notifying state itself is responsible for that situation. To permit it to do so would deprive interested third parties of the procedural guarantees conferred upon them by Article 93(2) of the Treaty (now Article 88(2) EC: the Commission would be allowed to rely on the conduct or negligence of the notifying Member State in order to thwart the purpose of Article 93(3) of the Treaty (now Article 88(3) EC, which requires it to initiate the formal examination procedure, and the Member State would be allowed to evade its duty of genuine cooperation."[161]

Equally, the Commission may open the formal investigation procedure when it considers that the aid can be authorised only with conditions. In this respect, the Commission encourages notifying parties to enter into preliminary contacts with the Commission officials, which very often lead to the proposals being altered to make them eligible for authorisation, thus avoiding the initiation of formal proceedings.

Article 6 of the Procedural Regulation indicates that the very aim of the decision to initiate proceedings is to summarise the relevant issues of fact and law, to include a preliminary assessment of the Commission as to the aid character of the proposed measure and to set out the doubts as to the compati-

---

[159] Case C 225/91, *Matra v Commission*, 1993 ECR I-3203, at paras. 33-39.

[160] Case T-73/98, *Société Chimique Prayon-Rupel SA v Commission*, 2001 ECR II-867, at para. 93.

[161] Ibid. at para. 100.

bility of the measure with the common market. Thus, the initiation decision constitutes a preparatory measure and its classification of the aid could not have any legal consequences that could be challenged before the courts pursuant to Article 230 EC. The CFI has confirmed the above in the *Territorio Histórico de Álava and Others v Commission* case by stating:

> "It follows that the classification of a measure as state aid in a decision to initiate the formal investigation procedure is merely provisional. The very aim of initiating the procedure is to enable the Commission to obtain all the views it needs in order to be able to adopt a definite decision on the point (...)."[162]

However, the CFI went on to draw a limitation of the judicial review of the Commission's decision to initiate proceedings:

> "In order to avoid confusion between the administrative and judicial proceedings, and to preserve the division of powers between the Commission and the Court, any review by the Court of First Instance of the legality of a decision to initiate the formal investigation procedure must necessarily be limited (...). The Court must in fact avoid giving a final ruling on questions on which the Commission has merely formed a provisional view. Thus, where in an action against a decision to initiate the formal investigation procedure the parties challenge the Commission's assessment of a measure as constituting state aid, review by the Court is limited to ascertaining whether or not the Commission has made a manifest error of assessment in forming the view that it was unable to resolve all the difficulties on that point during its initial examination of the measure concerned."[163]

Further, the Commission is not obliged to present a fully reasoned decision, when initiating proceedings, given that, as provided for in Article 6(1) of the Procedural Regulation, it is only obliged to give a preliminary assessment as to the character of the aid measure in question.[164]

The Commission cannot open formal investigation procedures to certain agricultural aid, even if it considers that the notified aid is incompatible with the common market, but can only make recommendations.[165]

---

[162] Joined Cases T-346/99, T-347/99 and T-348/99, *Territorio Histórico de Álava and Others v Commission*, ECR 2002 II-4259, at para. 28.

[163] Ibid. at paras. 44-45.

[164] Ibid. at paras. 98-100.

3.4.2 Conduct of the formal investigation procedure

The decision to open a formal investigation procedure is communicated to the Member state concerned by letter, whereas other Member States and interested parties are informed by notice in the Official Journal (OJ).

The above obligation stems from Article 88(2) EC, as well as from Article 6(1) of the Procedural Regulation, which particularly reads that the decision to initiate proceedings shall call upon the Member State concerned and upon other interested parties to submit their comments within a prescribed period. Given that it is in the interests of the Member States, of the recipient firms or of the Commission that the time, which elapses between the initiation and the final decision should be the shortest possible, the Commission instructs Member States to submit their comments, in full, within one month.[166] If it should prove necessary for Member States or other interested parties to supply oral observations to the Commission, the meetings for this purpose must be held within three months, at the latest, of receipt of the letter stating that the procedure has been initiated.

The Member State concerned, pursuant to Article 6(2) of the Procedural Regulation is also given the possibility to reply to the comments submitted by the other Member States or interested parties within a prescribed period, which shall normally not exceed one month. In duly justified cases, the Commission may extend the prescribed period.

There are no absolute time limits to the Commission's investigation although it is expected to be concluded promptly within an 18-month period, as provided for in Article 7(6) of the Procedural Regulation. This time limit however may be extended by common agreement between the Commission and the Member State concerned. The time length of the investigation depends on whether the Commission initiates the procedure for detailed investigation, invites interested parties to express their views and receives

---

165 Under Article 4 of Council Regulation (EEC) No. 26/62 applying certain rules of competition to production of and trade in agricultural products, only Article 93(1) of the Treaty (now Article 88(1) EC) and the first sentence of Article 93(3) of the Treaty (now Article 88(3) EC) apply to aid granted for certain agricultural products to which the Council has not yet made all the provisions of Articles 87 and 88 EC applicable under Article 36 EC (OJ C30/993, 20/04/1962). Therefore, the Commission is hindered to oppose various trade distorting aid plans, even if applied to intra-community trade, when these plans refer to aid for agricultural products for which no market organisation exists, such as potatoes other than starch potatoes, horsemeat, honey, coffee, alcohol of agricultural origin and vinegar derived from alcohol and cork (see XXth Report on Competition Policy, 1990 at p. 195). A similar situation is covered by Council Regulation (EEC) 706/73 concerning the Community arrangements applicable to the Channel Islands and the Isle of Man for trade in agricultural products (OJ L68, 15/03/1973).

166 Letter reference SG(87) D/5540 of 30/4/1987.

their comments in due time.

Unless the aid proposal is withdrawn, the Commission can take the following decisions:

The Commission may decide that the proposed measure, where appropriate following modification by the Member State concerned, *does not constitute aid*, pursuant to Article 7(2) of the Procedural Regulation, the reason being that it does not satisfy the criteria of Article 87(1) EC, i.e. it is not granted by a Member State or through state resources; it does not confer an advantage to the recipients; it does not favour certain (selected) undertakings or economic activities; it does not affect trade between Member States; or it does not distort competition in the common market.

Where the Commission finds that, following modifications by the Member State concerned, if necessary, the doubts as to the compatibility of the notified measure with the common market have been removed, it must take *a positive decision* that the aid is compatible with the common market. This decision shall specify which exception under the Treaty has been applied (Article 7(3) of the Procedural Regulation).

Aid may also be approved on conditions stipulated by the Commission (*conditional decision*). That is, the Commission may request certain changes or may specify certain restrictions (e.g. on the type, amounts, beneficiaries, purposes or duration of the aid) or may define certain performance targets. It may also lay down obligations to enable compliance with the decision to be monitored (Article 7(4) of the Procedural Regulation). On average about 6% of all cases are approved conditionally by the Commission.[167] If the Member State concerned fails to comply with the conditional decision and the aid is granted without taking into account the conditions and/or obligations imposed, then the aid is considered as unlawful and the Commission or any other Member State can bring the case before the Community courts.

In this respect it should be noted that the majority of notified schemes are approved unconditionally by the Commission because they comply with the criteria stipulated in notices, guidelines and frameworks.

In all cases, the Commission requires regular reporting by the national authorities so that it can monitor the conditions under which aid is disbursed and the effects it has.

Finally, where the Commission finds that the notified aid is not compatible with the common market, it shall issue *a negative decision* that the aid shall not be put into effect (Article 7(5) of the Procedural Regulation). On average about 7% of all cases are held as incompatible with the common mar-

---

[167] See the Spring edition 2003 of the State Aid Scoreboard at: "http://europa.eu.int/comm/competition/state_aid/scoreboard/".

ket.[168] Failure of the Member State to comply with that decision, entitles the Commission and any other Member State to bring the case against the Member State concerned before the Community courts.

The Commission should give a satisfactory reasoning for its final decisions pursuant to Article 253 EC. As stated in *BA plc and Others v Commission*:

> "It is thus necessary to ascertain whether the statement of reasons in the contested decision indicates clearly and unequivocally the Commission's reasoning, particularly in view of the essential complaints concerning the assessment of the contested aid plan put to the Commission during the administrative procedure (...)."[169]

3.5 Revocation of a decision

According to Article 9 of the Procedural Regulation the Commission may, after having given the Member State concerned the opportunity to submit its comments, revoke its decision taken under the preliminary examination or the formal investigation procedure that the notified measure does not constitute aid or the positive or conditional decision declaring the notified measure compatible with the common market. The Commission can exercise that power in any case where the decision was based on incorrect information provided during the procedure, which was a determining factor for the decision. Before revoking the decision and taking a new decision, the Commission shall open the formal investigation procedure and shall invite the Member State concerned and other interested parties to submit their comments. If aid has already been granted, it must be considered as unlawful aid and the Commission shall adopt a decision requiring the Member State concerned to suspend it until it has taken a decision on the compatibility of the aid with the common market (Article 11(1)). In the case that the Commission finds that the notified and already granted aid is not compatible with the common market, it shall decide that the Member State concerned shall take all the necessary measures to recover the aid from the beneficiary (Article 14(1)).

---

168 Ibid.

169 Joined cases T-371/94 and T-394/94, *British Airways and Others and British Midland Airways v Commission,* 1998 ECR II-2405, at para. 96.

4. PROCEDURE REGARDING UNLAWFUL AID

4.1 The notion of unlawful aid

According to Article 1(f) of the Procedural Regulation, unlawful aid shall mean new aid put into effect in contravention of Article 88(3) EC, i.e. aid which has either not been notified and aid that has been put into effect when it is notified or after being notified but before the Commission reaches its final decision.

The mere fact that aid is unlawful does not mean that it is also incompatible with the common market.[170] On the contrary, the Commission is obliged to examine the compatibility of the aid with the common market, in accordance with the procedure laid down in Articles 88(2) and (3) EC.[171]

4.2 Procedure

The procedures for unlawful aid are similar to those of notified aid discussed in the previous sections, except in the following respects, which stem from the illegality of the aid and the potential damage that this may cause to competitors.

Given that notification has not taken place, the procedure commences either following a complaint from a third party or *ex officio*.

Further, as provided for in Article 10(3) of the Procedural Regulation, the Commission is empowered to issue *an information injunction*, where the Member State concerned does not provide the information requested within the prescribed period or it provides incomplete information. That injunction shall specify what information is required and prescribe an appropriate period within which it is to be supplied.

The Commission may also issue a *suspension injunction* requiring the Member State to suspend any unlawful aid until the Commission has taken a decision of the compatibility of the aid with the common market (Article 11(1) of the Procedural Regulation). The ECJ has ruled on the Commission's power to issue suspension injunction well before the latter's inclusion in the

[170] In *Italy v Commission,* Advocate General Warner argued that where aid was unlawfully introduced in breach of the requirements of Article 88(3) EC, the Commission should then be able to bring an action before the ECJ for failure of the Member State to comply with the above Article, and that it should not proceed to examine the compatibility or not of the aid measure with the common market. This view has not, however, been endorsed by the ECJ (cited above at No. 22, at p. 725).

[171] Case C-301/87, *France v Commission* (cited above at No. 20, at para. 20).

Procedural Regulation. Thus in the *France v Commission* case the ECJ particularly stated that:

> "Once it has established that aid has been granted or altered without notification, the Commission therefore has the power, after giving the Member State in question an opportunity to submit its comments on the matter, to issue an interim decision requiring it to suspend immediately the payment of such aid pending the outcome of the examination of the aid and to provide the Commission, within such period as it may specify, with all such documentation, information and data as are necessary in order that it may examine the compatibility of the aid with the common market."[172]

In addition, pursuant to paragraph 2 of Article 11 of the Procedural Regulation, the Commission may adopt a decision requiring the Member State to provisionally recover any unlawful aid until the Commission has taken a decision on the compatibility of the aid with the common market ("recovery injunction"). A provisional recovery injunction may be ordered only if the following criteria are fulfilled: according to an established practice there are no doubts about the aid character of the measure concerned; there is urgency to act and there is serious risk of substantial and irreparable damage to a competitor.

Before issuing the above suspension and recovery injunctions the Commission should give the Member State concerned the opportunity to submit its comments. If the Member State concerned fails to comply with these injunctions, the Commission is entitled, while carrying out the examination on the substance of the matter, to bring the matter directly before the Community courts by applying for a declaration that the failure to comply amounts to an infringement of the Treaty (Article 12 of the Procedural Regulation).[173]

4.3 Decisions of the Commission and recovery of aid

4.3.1 Decisions

As in the case of notified aid measures, the Commission may issue the following decisions with regard to unlawful aid: firstly, it may find that the measure does not constitute aid under Article 87(1) EC. Further, it may also decide that the aid measure is compatible with the common market either because it is covered by an authorised aid scheme or because it is eligible for exemption

---

[172] Ibid. at para. 19.

[173] See also ibid. at para. 23.

under Articles 87(2) and (3) EC. The Commission finally can open formal proceedings if the Member State fails to supply information within the prescribed period and may also issue an injunction.
If the Member State fails to reply to the information injunction, the Commission shall take the decision on the basis of the information available, including that information received from third parties in response to the public notice, which the Commission has communicated to the Member States.[174]

It is important to point out that in unlawful cases the Commission is not bound by any time-limits. Thus the two-month period for the preliminary examination does not apply in this respect nor is the Commission obliged to take a decision during the formal investigation procedure, as provided for in Article 7 of the Procedural Regulation, as soon as the doubts expressed have been removed.

4.3.2 Recovery of unnotified aid

In cases of unnotified aid and before the Commission decides as to the compatibility of the measure with the common market, the Commission may order a recovery injunction pursuant to Article 11(2) of the Procedural Regulation.

Unlike the national courts, the Commission cannot order state aid to be repaid solely on the ground that it has not been notified in accordance with Article 88(3) of the Treaty.[175] National courts must offer to individuals the certain prospect that all the appropriate conclusions will be drawn from an infringement of the last sentence of Article 88(3) of the Treaty, in accordance with their national law, as regards the validity of measures giving effect to the aid, the recovery of financial support granted in disregard of that provision and possible interim measures.[176] The initiation of procedure by the Commission under either Article 88(2) or 88(3) EC does not relieve national courts of their duty to safeguard rights of individuals in the event of a breach of the requirement to give prior notification.[177] Therefore, the public authorities granting the aid, as well as any other interested parties, such as the competitors of the beneficiaries of the aid concerned who stand to suffer loss due to

---

174 Case C-364/90, Italy v Commission, 1993 ECR I-2097, at paras. 20-22 and 33-35. Case T-274/01, Valmont v Commission, paras 30 and 53-58.

175 Case C-301/87, *France v Commission* (cited above at No. 20, at paras. 19-22); Case C-142/87 *Belgium v Commission* (cited above at No. 69, at paras. 15-20); and Case C-354/90, *FNCEPA v France*, 1991 ECR I-5505, at para. 13.

176 Ibid. Case C-354/90 *FNCEPA v France,* at para. 12. See also Commission notice on cooperation between national courts and the Commission in the State aid field, OJ C312, 23/11/1995.

177 Case C-39/94, *SFEI v La Poste* (cited above at No. 47, at para. 44).

the grant of the illegal aid, may bring an action before the national court asking for the recovery of the sums granted on the basis of infringement of Article 88(3) EC, without it ruling on the compatibility of the measure.

The national authorities may also ask for the repayment of the sums granted without waiting for the Commission's decision and before bringing any action before national courts.

4.3.3 Recovery for incompatible unnotified aid

As has been mentioned above, if the Commission finds that the aid measure is incompatible with the common market, it shall issue a negative decision ordering the Member State concerning not to put the aid into effect.

In case of a negative decision taken for an unlawful measure, the Commission, may, pursuant to Article 14 of the Procedural Regulation, order the Member State concerned to take all the necessary measures to recover the aid from the beneficiary with interest. The Commission shall not require recovery of aid if that would be contrary to a general principle of Community law (Article 14(1)).[178] The case-law also has shown that there is the possibility that, in order to challenge its repayment, the recipients of unlawful aid may, in the procedure for the recovery of the aid, plead exceptional circumstances which could legitimately have given rise to a legitimate expectation that the aid was lawful. In *RSV v Commission,* it was held that the Commission's delay in giving the contested decision could in the case in point establish a legitimate expectation on the applicant's part so as to prevent the Commission from requiring the Netherlands Authorities to order the refund of the aid.[179]

However, as regards the applicant's alleged ignorance of the applicable rules, suffice it to recall that recipients of aid cannot be relieved of the obligation to keep themselves informed of the rules of Community law, otherwise the practical effect of Community law would be undermined. Nor can the fact that the applicant was not informed by the authorities of the administrative procedure, even if true, be regarded as an exceptional circumstance capable of giving rise to a legitimate expectation that the aid was lawful.[180]

The Commission can not require recovery of unlawful aid granted, if the

---

[178] See in this respect Case C-223/85, *RSV v Commission,* 1987 ECR 4617, where it follows that the Commission's delay in giving the contested decision could in the case in point establish a legitimate expectation on the applicant's part so as to prevent the Commission from requiring the Netherlands Authorities to order the refund of the aid (at para. 17).

[179] Ibid. at para 17. See also Case C-183/91, *Commission v Greece,* 1993 ECR I-3131, at para. 18.

[180] Case T-55/99, *CETM* v *Commission,* (cited above at No. 52, at para. 126-127). See also T-109/2001 *Fleuren Compost BV v Commission* of 14 January 2004, at paras 135-148 (not yet published).

limitation period of ten years, within which the Commission has the power to take the a decision has expired (Article 15 (1)). The limitation period shall begin on the day, which the unlawful aid is awarded to the beneficiary, either as individual aid or as aid under aid scheme. Aid with regard to which the limitation period has expired, shall be deemed to be existing aid (Article 15(3)).

Pursuant to Article 14(3), recovery of unlawful aid must be effected without delay and in accordance with the procedures under the national law of the Member State concerned, provided that they allow the immediate and effective execution of the Commission's decision. The question that arises in this respect is, what are the consequences and legal implications, when the national law makes the recovery impossible either because of political or legal difficulties?

It is established case law that the recovery must take place in accordance with the relevant procedural provisions of national law, subject however to the proviso that those provisions are to be applied in such a way that the recovery required by Community law is not rendered practically impossible.[181] In particular, the interest of the Community must always be taken into account in the application of the provision, which requires the various interests involved to be weighed up before a defective administrative measure is withdrawn.[182] In this connection, although, as above mentioned, there is the possibility for beneficiaries to rely on the principles of legitimate expectations and legal certainty, enshrined in national law, when arguing on the lawfulness of aid measure, it must be noted that, in view of the mandatory nature of the supervision of state aid by the Commission pursuant to Article 88 EC, they should not, in principle do that unless the aid has been granted in compliance with the procedure of the above mentioned Article. A diligent businessman should normally be able to determine whether that procedure has been followed.[183] Appendix XII below presents in a nutshell a diagrammatic preview of *Land Rheinland-Pfalz v Alcan Deutschland GmbH* case on the application of national law in cases of unlawful aid, where among others the interests of Community law need to be taken into account when recovery is claimed.[184]

The Commission decision to declare aid incompatible and order its recovery can be challenged before the Community courts, but this action does not have a suspensive effect, pursuant to Article 230 EC, although the Member State concerned may still apply for the suspension of the Commission decision pursuant to Article 242 EC. In this case, the Member State concerned

---

[181] Case C-142/87, *Belgium v Commission* (cited above at No. 69, at para. 61).

[182] Case C-94/87, *Commission v Germany,* 1989 ECR 175, at para 12.

[183] Case C-5/89, *Commission v Germany,* 1990 ECR I-3437, at para 12.

[184] Case C-24/95, 1997 ECR I-1591.

shall state the circumstances giving rise to urgency and the pleas of fact and law establishing a prima facie case for the interim measures applied for, as provided for in Article 83(2) of the Rules of Procedure of the ECJ and Article 104(2) of the Rules of Procedure of the CFI.[185] In the absence of any suspension order, the Member State is still obliged to recover the unlawful aid.[186]

5. PROCEDURE REGARDING MISUSE OF AID

According to Article 1(g) of the Procedural Regulation, misuse of aid shall mean aid used by the beneficiary in contravention of a decision authorising the aid, i.e. either under Article 4(3), that is to say a decision not to raise objections, or under Article 7(3) and (4), that is to say a positive or a conditional decision.

Aid is, therefore, misused when, for example, it is used for a different purpose than the one that it was granted for[187] or is used to benefit a different undertaking than the actual recipient.[188]

The procedure followed is the same as in unlawful aid, but the Commission should always open the formal investigation procedure, given that misuse of aid can only arise in the context of existing aid. The Commission may, thus, take a decision ordering the Member State concerned to suspend the aid measure until it decides on its compatibility with the common market, but it does not have the power to issue a recovery injunction. Where the Commission finds that the misuse of aid is incompatible with the common market, it shall require the Member State concerned to take all the necessary steps to recover the aid that has been misused.

6. PROCEDURE REGARDING EXISTING AID SCHEMES

6.1 Monitoring of existing aid under Article 88(1) EC

In accordance with Article 88(1) EC and Article 17 of the Procedural Regulation, the Commission shall, in cooperation with the Member States, keep

[185] Case C-278/00, *Greece v Commission*, 2000 ECR I-8787, at para. 27.

[186] Case 261/99, *Commission v France*, 2001 ECR I-2537, at para. 27.

[187] Commission Decision 1999/580/ECSC, *ESF Elbestahlwerk Feralpi GmbH*, OJ L220, 20/08/1999, where the Commission authorised investment aid but the beneficiary used it to cover operating costs.

[188] Commission Decision 2000/796/EC, *Compact Discs Albrechts GmbH*, OJ L318, 16/12/2000.

under constant review all systems of aid existing in those states and obtain from the Member States all the necessary information for the review.

The constant review of existing aid schemes is necessary because many of them were approved years ago at a time when the economic circumstances were different and when the Community market was more fragmented than is the case today. It may be, therefore, that the authorisation given by the Commission at the time is no longer justified.[189]

Where, thus, the Commission considers that an existing aid scheme is not, or is no longer, compatible with the common market, it shall inform the Member State concerned of its preliminary view and give the Member State concerned the opportunity to submit its comments within a period of one month or more in duly justified cases (Article 17(2) of the Procedural Regulation).

In the light of the information submitted by the Member State, the Commission, pursuant to Article 88(1) EC and Article 18 of the Procedural Regulation shall issue a recommendation proposing appropriate measures to the Member State concerned, if it concludes that the existing aid is not, or is not longer, compatible with the common market. The recommendation may propose in particular substantive amendment of the aid scheme, or introduction of procedural requirements or abolition of the aid scheme and it shall be reasoned.[190]

If the Member State concerned agrees to the recommendation proposed, it, according to Article 19(1) of the Procedural Regulation, shall be bound by its acceptance to implement it and the Commission closes the file with a decision, which is published in the OJ, pursuant to Article 26(1) of the Procedural Regulation. The Commission's recommendations are not, however, binding on Member States as a matter of general EC law pursuant to Article 249 EC.[191] Where, thus, the Member State concerned does not accept the proposed measures, and the Commission, having taken into account the arguments of the Member State concerned, still considers that those measures are necessary, it shall initiate proceedings under Article 88(2) EC. In that case, the appropriate proposed measures become binding following the Commission's final decision on the incompatibility. Of course, before the Commission has taken any decision, the Member State concerned may petition the Council, which may decide unanimously whether existing aid schemes are compatible with the common market. As already noted, however, this is rare.

---

[189] XXth Report on Competition Policy, 1991, at p.128.

[190] Case 173/73, *Italy v Commission* (cited above at No. 22, at para. 57).

[191] See also Cases T-132/96 and T-143/96, *Freistaat Sachsen v Commission*, 1999 ECR II-3663, at para. 209.

6.2 Review of existing aid schemes in particular sectors

The Commission may also use the Article 88(1) EC procedure in order to review existing aid schemes in all Member States at once. This may be the case where the Commission sees a need to tighten up the control of aid to particular sectors and issues guidelines and frameworks as appropriate measures[192] that the Member States have to comply with.

If the Member States agree with the new rules, they become binding. If, on the other hand, a Member State declines to comply with the proposed measures, the Commission will initiate proceedings under Article 88(2) EC in respect of relevant existing aid schemes in that Member State. The above was the case in the motor vehicle industry. Following the adoption of a framework in July 1997, all Member States had accepted it except Sweden. Accordingly, the Commission initiated proceedings in October 1997 against all existing Swedish schemes, which could be the basis for state aid in the motor vehicle sector as from 1 January 1998. During the proceedings the Swedish authorities accepted the Commission's position and the file was closed on 21 January1998.[193]

The Commission also carries out general reviews of policy on aid for particular purposes and announces new or codified rules on such aid without seeking immediate across-the-board changes in existing schemes to comply with the new rules but instead allowing a period of time for adjustment. In such a case, the Commission applies the rules to new or amended schemes as and when they are notified and at the same time reviews individually under Article 88(1) EC any existing schemes not renotified within a certain period. For such ruling the Commission does not ask for the Member States' consent under Article 88(1) EC, as the introduction of the rules does not of itself involve changes to existing schemes, but they are applied to each scheme individually afterwards.[194]

---

192 This term must be interpreted in a broader sense as covering proposals also in the form of frameworks and guidelines directed to all Member States.

193 XXVIIIth Report on Competition Policy, 1998, at p. 227. See also XXth Report on Competition Policy, 1991, at p. 157-159.

194 See for example Framework on State Aid to Shipbuilding, OJ C317, 30/12/2003; Also Communication from the Commission, Multisectoral framework on regional aid for large investment projects, OJ C70, 19/03/2002.

7. INTERESTED PARTIES AND THE RIGHTS OF DEFENCE

7.1 The legal provisions

According to Article 1(h) of the Procedural Regulation, interested parties in the EC state aid proceedings shall mean any Member State and any person, undertaking or association of undertakings whose interests might be affected by the granting of aid, in particular the beneficiary of the aid, competing undertakings and trade associations. Customers, suppliers and employees, including representatives of the employees of the beneficiaries may also be considered as interested parties.[195]

The Procedural Regulation has codified in two Articles the rights of the interested parties in the procedure. These are as follows:

i. The right to submit comments within a prescribed period on the Commission's decision to open a formal investigation procedure (Article 6(1));[196]
ii. The right of the interested party which has submitted such comments to be sent a copy of the Commission's final decision (Article 20(1));
iii. The right to inform the Commission of any alleged unlawful or misuse of aid and the right to be informed by the Commission, if the latter considers that on the basis of the information in its possession there are insufficient grounds for taking such a view on the case (Article 20(2));
iv. The right to receive a copy of the Commission's final decision, where the Commission takes such a decision on a case concerning the subject matter of the complaint and information supplied (Article 20(2)); and
v. The right to receive at its request a copy of any decision taken by the Commission in the proceedings (Article 20(3)).

Further, as regards actions against other Member States, in accordance with Article 88(2) EC, where the Member State concerned does not comply with the Commission's decision within the prescribed time, the Commission or any interested Member State may refer the matter to the ECJ direct. Alternatively, pursuant to Article 227 EC, an interested Member State, which considers that the Member State that granted the aid has failed to fulfil its obligation under the Treaty, may bring the matter before the ECJ. In this case, the interested Member State should firstly bring the matter before the Commission. The latter is obliged to deliver a reasoned opinion within three months of the date on which the matter was brought before it, after each of the

---

[195] Case T-189/97, *Comité d' Entreprise de la Société Française de Production v Commission*, 1998 ECR II-335, at para. 41.

[196] This right also stems from Article 88(2) EC.

states concerned has submitted its own observations on the other party's case both orally and in writing. In the absence of such an opinion, the interested Member State is empowered to bring the matter before the ECJ. Interested parties other than Member States, such as the beneficiaries of the aid or their competitors, have no right under the Treaty to bring actions before the ECJ against the Member State concerned for failure to comply with the Commission's decision or for implementing an unlawful aid measure.

With regard to actions against the Commission's decisions, Article 230(2) EC provides that the Member State concerned as well as any other interested Member States may challenge acts of the Commission before the ECJ. Likewise, according to Article 230(4), any other natural or legal persons may institute proceedings against the Commission decision, which although in the form of regulation or a decision addressed to another person, is of direct and individual concern to them. In addition, should the Commission, in infringement of the Treaty, fail to act, an action may be brought in accordance with Article 232 EC, in order to have the infringement established. In this respect, it should be pointed out that for actions brought by a Member State the competent court is the ECJ, whereas the CFI is competent for actions brought by the individual undertakings or other natural or legal persons.

7.2 The case law

Case law over the last years has been particularly rich as regards the procedural rules and the rights of interested parties/third parties in the EC State aid proceedings.

The administrative procedure regarding aid is opened only against the Member State concerned. Undertakings that receive aid and the local authorities within that state which grant the aid are considered, in the same way as competitors of the recipients of the aid, only to be "interested parties" in this procedure.[197]

Given the essentially bilateral nature of the various procedures laid down in Article 88, which are based principally on a dialogue between the Member State concerned and the Commission, the rights which third parties are recognised as having in the state aid field are necessarily more restricted than the rights under Article 81 and 82 EC Treaty. Case law has shown that third party rights are essentially relevant in the context of the procedure under Article 88(2) EC and the formal investigation procedure.[198]

---

[197] Case T-158/96, *Acciaierie di Bolzano v Commission*, 1999 ECR II-3927, at para. 42.
[198] XXVIIIth Report on Competition Policy, 1998, at p. 104.

It is settled law that in the context of an examination under Article 88(2) EC, the Commission is required to give notice to the parties concerned to submit their comments. In the *Cook v Commission* and *Matra v Commission* cases, the ECJ confirmed the circumstances in which the Commission is obliged to open proceedings under Article 88(2) EC in order to allow interested third parties, generally competitors, to comment on the aid proposals.[199]

With regard to that duty, the ECJ has ruled that the publication of a notice in the OJ is an appropriate means of informing all the parties concerned that a procedure has been initiated, while also pointing out that the sole aim of this communication is to obtain from persons concerned all information required for the guidance of the Commission with regard to its future action.[200]

However, the above does not apply to preliminary examination. When the compatibility of the aid with the common market can be established without the opening of the formal investigation procedure, it does not appear that third parties have a right to be heard in the procedure. This has also been confirmed by the ECJ in a number of judgements.[201]

Regarding access of interested parties to the file, no relevant provision exists either in the Procedural Regulation or the EC Treaty. The Commission has also refused this on the grounds that the legal party to the proceedings is the Member State. This practice was explicitly confirmed by the CFI in the *Ufex v Commission* case, where it was stated that in view of the limited nature of their rights to participation and to information, the Commission is not obliged to forward to interested parties the observations or information received from the Member States concerned.[202]

The same also applies to the right for an oral hearing. It has been argued that, although there is no legal provision on such a right, the principle of the rights of defence should entitle at least the beneficiary of aid to request a hearing.[203]

Therefore, it follows that, far from enjoying the same rights of defence as those which individuals against whom a procedure has been instituted are recognised as having, the parties concerned have only the right to be involved in the administrative procedure to the extent appropriate in the light of the cir-

---

199 Case C-198/91, *William Cook v Commission,* 1993 ECR I-1719, at para. 30 and Case C-225/91 *Matra v Commission* (cited above at No. 152, at paras 33-36).

200 Case 323/82, *Intermill v Commission*, 1984 ECR 3809, at paras. 16-17. See also Case 70/72, *Commission v Germany,* 1973 ECR, at para. 19 and Case T-266/94, *Skibsværftsforeningen and Others v Commission*, 1996 ECR II-1399, at para. 256.

201 Case C-225/91 *Matra v Commission* (cited above at No. 152, at para. 54); Case 84/82, *Germany v Commission,* 1984 ECR 1451, at para. 13.

202 Case T-613/97, *Ufex v Commission* (cited above at No. 131, at para. 90).

203 P. Bentley, *State Aid, Subsidies and Complainants*, 1990 EBLR at p. 94.

cumstances of the case.[204] The recent judgement of the CFI in *Fleuren Compost BV v Commission,* has confirmed all the above mentioned:

> "The Court has held that publication of a notice in the Official Journal of the European Communities is an appropriate means of informing all the parties concerned that a procedure has been initiated (…). That communication is intended to obtain from the persons concerned all the information needed to guide the Commission with regard to its future action (…). Such a procedure also guarantees to the other Member States and the sectors concerned an opportunity to make their views known (…). However, the procedure for reviewing state aid is, in view of its general scheme, a procedure initiated in respect of the Member State responsible, in light of its Community obligations, for granting the aid (…).
> Under the procedure for reviewing state aid, interested parties other than the Member state concerned have only the role mentioned in paragraph 41 above and, in that regard, they cannot themselves lay claim to an exchange of arguments with the Commission such as that initiated in regard to that Member State (…).
> Of the interested parties, the recipient of the aid does not play a special role pursuant to any provision governing the procedure for the review of state aid. The procedure for the review of state aid is not a procedure initiated against the recipient or recipients of aid by virtue of which it or they could rely on rights as extensive as the rights of the defence as such (…).
> Therefore, since the decision to initiate the procedure provided for in Article 88(2) EC contains an adequate preliminary analysis by the Commission setting out the reasons for its doubts regarding the compatibility of the aid in question with the common market, it is for the Member State concerned and, where appropriate, the recipient of the aid to adduce evidence to show that the aid is compatible with the common market and, if necessary, to plead specific circumstances relating to recovery of the aid already paid should the Commission require its repayment."[205]

8. STATE AID MONITORING

The Commission monitors state aid measures either through the annual reports submitted by Member States or through on site monitoring inspec-

---

[204] Joined cases T-371/94 & T-394/94 (cited above at No. 162, at para 60).

[205] Case T-109/01, *Fleuren Compost BV v Commission,* 2004, at paras. 41-46 (not yet reported).

tions. According to Article 21 of the Procedural Regulation, Member States submit to the Commission annual reports on all approved aid schemes.[206] Where, despite a reminder, the Member State concerned fails to submit an annual report, the Commission may propose appropriate measures with regard to the aid scheme concerned. The new Implementing Regulation provides in Articles 5, 6 and 7 specific conditions on the form and content, transmission, publication and status of the annual reports.

Where the Commission has serious doubts as to whether decisions not to raise objections, positive decisions or conditional decisions with regard to individual aid are being complied with, the Member State concerned, after having been given the opportunity to submit its comments, shall allow the Commission to undertake on-site monitoring pursuant to Article 22 of the Procedural Regulation. Commission authorised officials and experts, after having informed the Member State concerned, in good time and in writing, of the on-site monitoring visit and of their identities, are empowered, in order to verify compliance with the decision concerned, to enter any premises and land of the undertakings concerned, to ask for oral explanations on the spot, to examine books and other business records and take or demand copies. Where an undertaking opposes a monitoring visit ordered by a Commission decision, the Member State concerned should afford the necessary assistance to the officials and experts authorised by the Commission to enable them to carry out the monitoring visit. However, the Commission has not so far exercised these powers.

---

[206] See for example Framework on State Aid to Shipbuilding (cited above at No. 187, at para. 28).

Further Reading

The website of DG Competition of the European Commission provides access to all official documents (Regulations, guidelines, frameworks, notices, etc.). See: "http://europa.eu.int/comm/competition/index_en.html"

Detailed analysis and critique of state aid rules, procedures and practice can be found in the following textbooks and journal articles:

GENERAL TEXTBOOKS:

C. Quigley & A. Collins, *EC State Aid Law and Policy*, (Oxford: Hart Publishing, 2003).

S. Bilal & P. Nicolaides (eds.), *Understanding State Aid Policy in the European Community: Perspectives on Rules and Practice*, (The Hague: Kluwer Publishers, 1999).

R. D'Sa, *European Community Law on State Aid*, (London: Sweet & Maxwell, 1998).

C. Baudenbacher, *A Brief Guide to European State Aid Law*, (London: Kluwer Law International, 1997).

A. Evans, *European Community Law of State Aid*, (Oxford: Clarendon, 1997).

In addition, below we provide references to some of our own papers that deal in more detail with particular issues concerning state aid.

P. Nicolaides and M. Kekelekis, When do Firms in Trouble Escape From State Aid Rules?, *European State Aid Law Quarterly*, 2005.

P. Nicolaides and M. Kekelekis, An Economic Analysis of EC Guidelines on

State Aid for the Rescue and Restructuring of Companies in Difficulty, *Intereconomics*, 2004.

P. Nicolaides and M. Kekelekis, An Assessment of EC State Aid Policy on Rescue and Restructuring of Companies in Difficulty, *European Competition Law Review*, 2004.

P. Nicolaides, Re-Introducing the Market in the "Market Economy Investor" Principle, *European State Aid Law Quarterly*, 2003.

P. Nicolaides, Compensation for Public Service Obligations: The Floodgates of State Aid? *European Competition Law Review*, 2003.

P. Nicolaides, Regional State Aid, *European State Aid Law Quarterly*, 2003.

P. Nicolaides, Decentralised State Aid Control in an Enlarged European Union: Feasible, Necessary or Both? *World Competition*, 2003.

P. Nicolaides, Control of State Aid in the EU: Compliance, Sanctions and Rational Behaviour, *World Competition*, 2002.

P. Nicolaides, The Distortive Effects of Compensatory Aid Measures: A Note on the Economics of the "Ferring" Judgement, *European Competition Law Review*, 2002.

P. Nicolaides, Operating Aid and Fiscal Aid in the EC: A Critical Review of Current Practice, *World Competition*, 2001.

P. Nicolaides and S. Bilal, An Appraisal of EC Rules on State Aid, *Journal of World Trade*, 1999.

APPENDIX I
A Diagrammatic Presentation of Regulation 659/99

I. Before Commission Decides

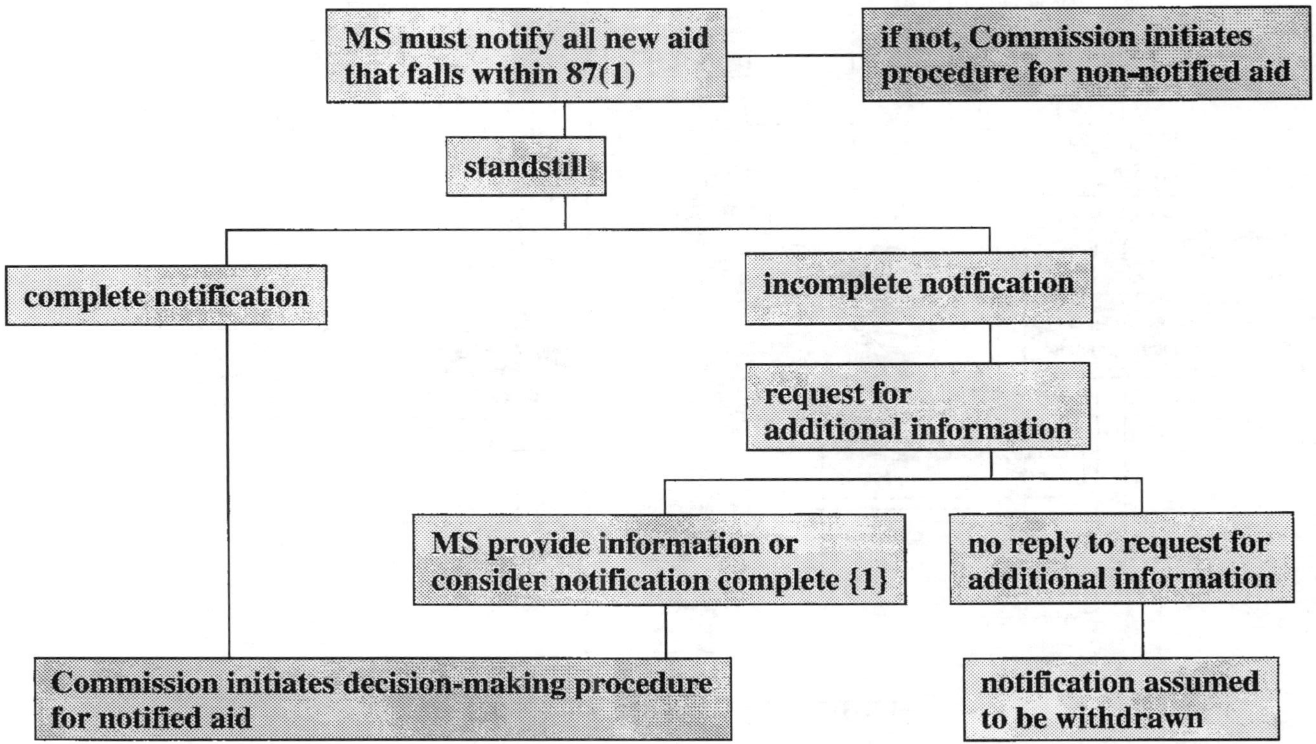

II. Decision Making Procedures

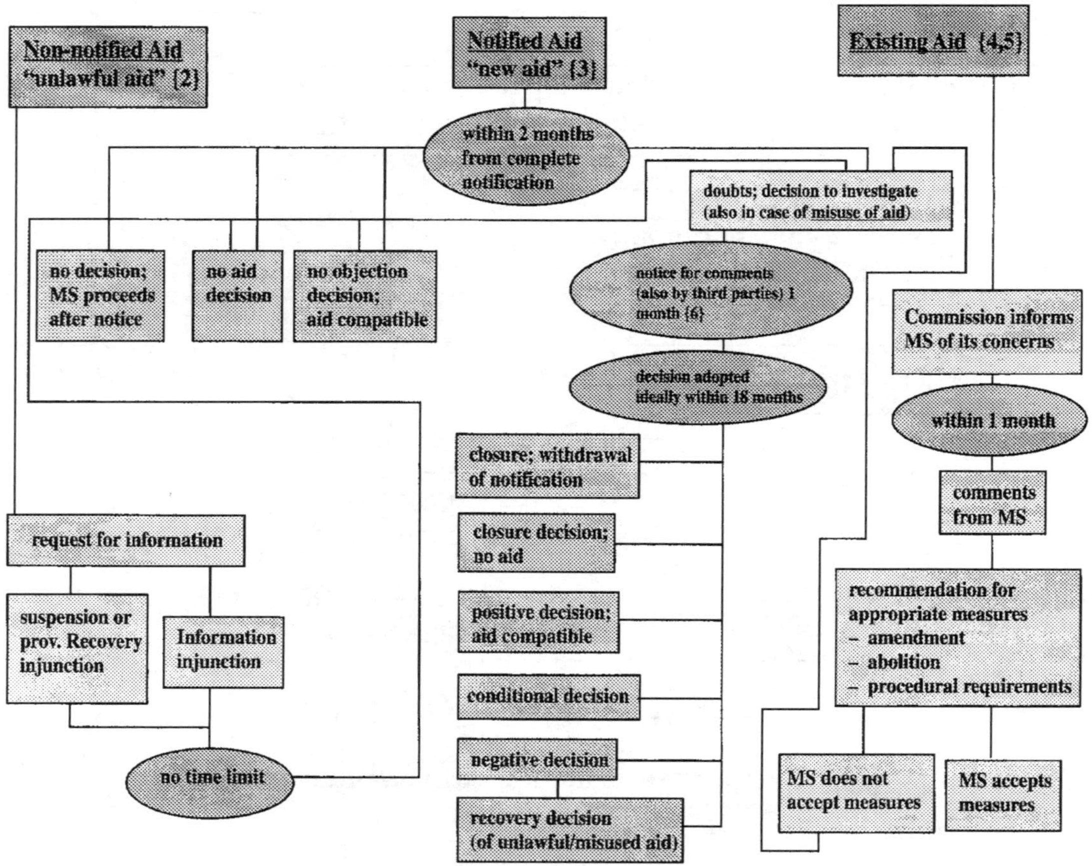

III. After Commission Decides

Publication in OJ of decision in all languages;
(copies of decision given to interested parties that provided comments and, if requested, to other interested parties)
Summary notices on compatible aid and cases of no objections

MS submit annual reports on all existing aid (including authorised aid)

Commission may undertake on site monitoring

Commission may adopt implementing provisions on:
- **notifications**
- **annual reports**
- **time limits**
- **interest rates**

Advisory Committee on State Aid

Main Provisions of Regulation 794/2004
(OJ L140, 30/04/2004)

Notifications (Articles 2, 3 & 4)

- New aid has to be notified on specified new forms.
- Forms have to be transmitted to the Commission by the Permanent Representations.
- Forms have to be submitted electronically as of 1/1/2006.
- Simplified notification form to be used for alterations to existing aid when:
  - the increase in the budget of authorised scheme exceeds 20% (if the increase is less than 20% then there is no alteration of existing aid);
  - extension of an authorised scheme for up to 6 years;
  - stricter criteria are used (e.g. reduction of aid intensity or eligible expenses).
- In simplified procedures the Commission will try to reply within one month.

Annual reports (Articles 5, 6 & 7) & time limits and periods (Article 9)

- Annual reports are prepared for each calendar year in which a scheme applies in accordance with a standardised reporting format.
- Annual reports are submitted to the Commission no later than 30 June.
- Time limits are calculated as in Regulation 1182/71.

Interest rate to be applied for aid recovery (Articles 9, 10 & 11)

- The rate is fixed each year for each or more member states.
- The rate is calculated on the basis of average 5-year inter-bank swap rates during September, October & November of the previous year plus 75 points.
- The Commission may increase that rate by more than 75 points and may in the absence of reliable data or in exceptional circumstances fix a rate by a different method.
- The rate is applied as of the date that the unlawful aid is granted and to has to be compounded.
- That rate applies throughout the recovery period or is recalculated every 5 years if the recovery period exceeds 5 years.

APPENDIX II
Permitted Rates of Aid Intensity
(as % of eligible costs)

Type of aid	Standard rates	87(3)(a) area	87(3)(c) area
Regional	--	50/ram	20/ram
-- sme		+15	+10
Environmental	30/40	+10	+5
-- sme	+10		
R&D	25/50/100	+10	+5
-- sme	+10		
SME Regulation	7.5/15	+15	+10
Training Regulation	25/50	+10	+5
-- sme	+10/20		
Employment Reg.	--	ram*	ram*
-- sme	7.5/15	+15	+10

Note: "ram" is the regional aid map approved by the Commission for each member state. It specifies the maximum rates of aid intensity that may be granted in each region of each member state. The regional aid guidelines define general ceilings of 20% and 50% but the applicable rates are those in the ram.

* the employment regulation allows aid to large companies (i.e. non-SMEs) only in assisted areas up to the rate determined by the relevant ram.

APPENDIX III
Regional Aid and Multisectoral Framework

1. Regional state aid

The regional aid Guidelines serve primarily three functions: to identify the various categories of eligible areas, to determine the allowable instruments of state aid and to modulate the intensity of state aid that is received by different eligible areas.[207]

With respect to the definition of eligible areas, the intention of the Commission was to ensure as much as possible coincidence between 87(3)(a) areas and Objective 1 regions under the structural funds and between 87(3)(c) areas and Objective 2 regions.[208] The total share of the EU population eligible to receive regional aid was fixed by the Commission at 42.7%.

Eligible population for regional state aid, 2000 - 2006

	% of eligible population	Type of 87(3) area
Belgium	30.9	c
Denmark	17.1	c
Germany	34.9	a + c
Greece	100.0	a
Spain	79.2	a + c
France	36.7	a + c
Ireland	100.0	a + c
Italy	43.6	a + c
Luxembourg	32.0	c
Netherlands	15.0	c
Austria	27.5	a + c
Portugal	100.0	a + c
Finland	42.2	a + c

[207] OJ C212, 12/08/1988.
[208] Commission Notice in OJ C16, 21/01/1999.

	% of eligible population	Type of 87(3) area
Sweden	15.9	c
United Kingdom	28.7	a + c
EC	*42.7*	
10 new Member States	100.0	a + c [c] areas are: Cyprus Czech Republic (Prague) Slovakia (Bratislava)

After the enlargement of the EU to 25 Member States on 1 May 2004, the percentage of total population of the EU of 25 that is eligible for state aid has increased to 52.1%. The table at the end of this Appendix shows the eligible population of each of the new Member States and the proposed population coverage for the period 2006 to 2013.

With respect to the instruments of state aid, the Guidelines permit only two instruments: investment and job creation linked to investment. They also exceptionally allow operating aid but only for 87(3)(a) areas and only when it is temporary, degressive over time and clearly linked to offsetting regional handicaps (by a separate Notice, the Commission has in the meantime allowed operating aid on a permanent basis to the outermost regions of the EU and for the partial compensation of transport costs in the low density regions; i.e. the polar regions of Finland and Sweden).[209]

Investment aid is restricted to initial or extension investment. Replacement investment is not allowed. Subsidised assets must also be kept by the beneficiary firm for at least five years. Aid for job creation is restricted only to jobs that are linked to either initial or extension investment. The jobs must be made available within three years of the investment and must also be maintained for at least five years.

It is worth noting that the recently adopted Regulation on Employment aid 2204/2002, has severed the link between investment and aid for jobs.[210] Under that Regulation firms may receive aid for hiring more people as a result of expansion in their operations rather than as net addition to their asset base. Moreover, the Regulation requires beneficiary firms to keep new employees for a minimum of three years instead of five, while SMEs can keep them only for two years.

Lastly, the Guidelines set maximum ceilings for the intensity of granted aid. Intensity is measured as a percentage of aid in relation to the eligible costs. It is important to understand that while the Guidelines define maximum rates, the rates which are applicable to each region are those approved by the Commission individually and included in each member state's regional aid map. The table below shows the rates

[209] Commission Notice in OJ C285, 09/09/2000.
[210] OJ L337, 13/12/2002.

defined in the Guidelines. As can be seen, there is considerable variation across regions.

Regional aid: Maximum aid intensities
(amount of aid as % of eligible cost)

	87(3)(a) area	87(3)(c) area
Maximum rate – if regional GDP > 60% of EU average – if GDP > EU average & unemployment < EU average – if next to 87(3)(a) area	50 40 - -	20 - 10 20
Outermost region – if regional GDP > 60% of EU average – if GDP > EU average & unemployment < EU average	65 50 -	30 - 20
Low density region – if regional GDP > 60% of EU average – if GDP > EU average & unemployment < EU average	50 40 -	30 - 20
SME	+ 15	+ 10

NGE v GGE

An unusual feature of the regional guidelines is that they express the various ceilings of allowable aid in net grant equivalent. Member States, however, have to notify in terms of gross grant equivalent. The difference between the two is that the former excludes any tax on the aid grants that may have to be paid by the recipient undertakings. The following example illustrates this difference. Suppose a project totalling € 1,000,000 is being funded in an 87(3)(c) area with ceiling of 20%.

- Aid ceiling (NGE): 20%
- Eligible investment: € 1,000,000
- Taxable grant: € 240,000
- Tax rate: 25%
- GGE: 240,000/1,000,000 = 24%
- Tax payable: € 240,000 x 0.25 = € 60,000
- NGE: (240,000 – 60,000)/1,000,000 = **18%**

Cumulation

For the purpose of complying with the ceilings defined in the regional aid map of each Member State, the Guidelines require that all public funds including Community sources must fall below the allowable rates of aid intensity. In case a project receives support from the structural funds, it must in addition comply with Regulation 1260/99 concerning the application of those funds. In particular, Art. 29(4)(b) of the Regulation stipulates that the rate of EC co-financing of investment in firms is maximum

35% of total costs in Objective 1 regions and maximum 15% of total costs in Objective 2 regions.

Example of cumulation of national funds with ERDF money

Source of Funds	Classification of funds	Recipient of Funds
Case I *Ministry of Public Works* **ERDF**	*National funds: no state aid* **EC funds: no state aid**	Infrastructural project [e.g. road]
Case II *Ministry of Industry [€ 5 mn]* **ERDF [€ 15 mn]** Company [€ 80 mn]	*National funds: state aid* **EC funds: no state aid** Public funds that have to be cumulated resulting in: = aid intensity: 20% = EC assistance: 15%	Company that undertakes investment in an 87(3)(c) area with aid intensity of 20%

2. The Multisectoral Framework

An innovation of the Commission for the present financial perspective has been the introduction of rules of the individual notification and the reduction of aid to large projects. These rules were introduced in 1998 by the "Multisectoral Framework." A new Framework partially came into effect since the expiry of the Treaty on the European Coal and Steal Community in July 2002 and is in full force since 1 January 2004.[211]

The Multisectoral Framework reduces allowable aid intensities for large projects because such projects have a bigger impact on competition, they are more likely to be undertaken by multinational companies which are less affected by regional handicaps (e.g. they have access to capital markets or cutting-edge technology) and because these companies can exert much more pressure on regional and local authorities to grant aid up to the permitted ceiling. The adjustment is made as follows

[211] OJ C263, 01/11/2003.

Multisectoral Framework: Maximum aid intensities for large projects

Eligible expenditure	Adjusted regional ceiling (R)
A: up to € 50 million B: € 50 – 100 million C: over € 100 million	100% of ceiling 50% of ceiling 34% of ceiling
Formula for adjusting ceiling: **Maximum eligible aid = R(A + 0.5B + 0.34C)**	

For example, a project costing € 160 million in area with a 25% ceiling can obtain aid up to € 23.85 million. This is equivalent to aid intensity of only 14.9%.

Notification is required for every case where the amount of aid exceeds the aid that corresponds to an investment costing € 100 million. It follows that notifiable projects vary from area to area depending both on the size of the project and also on the aid intensity allowed for each area.

For example, in an area with aid ceiling of 20%, a factory costing € 250 million can benefit from aid up to a maximum of € 25.2 million. Since, however, in the same area an investment costing € 100 million can obtain € 15 million of aid, any amount of aid for that factory that exceeds € 15 million will have to be notified individually. In other words, that factory will have to obtain aid of less than to € 15 million to escape notification. This means that the intensity of that aid will have to be less than 6% (= 15/250), even though in principle the rate is 20% for that area.

3. Impact on state aid of the proposed reform of cohesion policy and structural funds

On 18 February 2004 the Commission published its 3rd Cohesion Report which contains its proposals for reform of structural funds for the next financial perspective that will span the period between 2007 and 2013. Because the reform affects also the eligibility of regions for state aid, the Report also puts forth ideas for adjustment of regional aid maps and aid intensities.

A summary of the proposals is provided in the tables below. The first table shows the regions that will be eligible for assistance, the second table shows the new aid intensities while the third table shows the percentage of population in each Member State that will be eligible for support. Please note that if the Commission proposals are accepted, then the aid intensities allowed by the SME Regulation 70/2001 will have to be raised.

Table 1

Assisted areas under the proposed revision of regional guidelines	Treaty status
Areas with a GDP per capita level of less than 75% of the average for the whole EU25.	Article 87(3)(a)
Areas with a GDP per capita above 75% of the average GDP of the newly enlarged EU, but below 75% of the average for the old EU15 ("statistical effect" areas).	Article 87(3)(c)
Regions losing Article 87(3)(a) status and also not qualifying as statistical effect areas as a result of economic growth ("economic growth" areas)	Article 87(3)(c)
Certain other areas qualifying on grounds of remoteness, (such as Reunion and the Azores) or on grounds of low population density (such as northern Sweden and Finland).	Article 87(3)(c)

Table 2

Enterprises	Large Enterprises	Medium-sized Enterprises	Small Enterprises
Article 87(3)(a) region ≤ 45% GDP	40%	50%	60%
Article 87(3)(a) region ≤ 60% GDP	35%	45%	55%
Article 87(3)(a) region ≤ 75% GDP	30%	40%	50%
Article 87(3)(c) outermost GDP > 60% / GDP < 60%	40%	50%	60%
Article 87(3)(c) "statistical effect" (dates when rates are applicable)	1/07, 1/10, 1/12 30, 22.5, 15%	1/07, 1/10, 1/12 40, 32.5, 25%	1/07, 1/10, 1/12 50, 42.5, 35%
Article 87(3)(c) low density	20%	30%	40%
Article 87(3)(c) economic development	15%	25%	35%
Non-assisted areas	0	10%	20%

Table 3

EU Member State	Current % population in assisted areas	% population in assisted areas under Commission proposals
Austria	27.50%	3.40%
Belgium	30.90%	16.80%
Cyprus	20.0%	0.00% [excluding Northern Cyprus]
Czech Republic	100.0%	88.20%
Denmark	17.10%	0.0%
Estonia	10.0%	100.0%
Finland	42.20%	13.10%
France	36.70%	2.80%
Germany	34.90%	16.80%
Greece	100.0%	100.0%
Hungary	100.0%	100.0%
Ireland	100.0%	26.40%
Italy	43.60%	33.20%
Latvia	100.0%	100.0%
Lithuania	100.0%	100.0%
Luxembourg	32.0%	0.0%
Malta	100.0%	100.0%
Netherlands	15.0%	0.0%
Poland	100.0%	100.0%
Portugal	100.0%	74.70%
Slovakia	100.0%	88.90%
Slovenia	100.0%	100.0%
Spain	79.20%	58.20%
Sweden	15.90%	10.0%

EU Member State	Current % population in assisted areas	% population in assisted areas under Commission proposals
UK	30.90%	9.10%

APPENDIX IV
Training Aid: Regulation 68/2001

1. Introduction

The Regulation covers all sectors, including agriculture and fisheries but excepting coal mining. The Regulation is in force for five years thus aid should not be extended beyond December 2006.

2. Definitions

- **Specific training:** shall mean training involving tuition directly and principally applicable to the employee's present or future position in the assisted firm and providing qualifications which are not or only to a limited extent transferable to other firms or fields of work.
- **General training:** shall mean training involving tuition which is not applicable only or principally to the employee's present or future position in the assisted firm, but which provides qualifications that are largely transferable to other firms or fields of work and thereby substantially improve the employability of the employees. Training shall be considered "general" if, for example:
  - It is jointly organised by different independent enterprises, or if the employees of different enterprises may avail themselves of the training,
  - It is recognised, certified or validated by public authorities or bodies or by other bodies or institutions on which a Member State or the Community has conferred the necessary powers.

3. Permitted intensities

	SME	Large Enterprise	Article 87 (3)(a)	Article 87 (3)(c)
Specific Training (Gross aid as percentage of eligible cost)	35%	25%	+10%	+5%
General Training (Gross aid as percentage of eligible cost)	70%	50%	+10%	+5%
The overall ceilings shall be increased by 10% for disadvantaged workers				

Eligible costs: trainer's fee and expenses (travel, material) and trainees' training time and expenses

Where aid is granted in the shipping sector, aid intensity is 100% for either specific or general training, if the trainee is not a crew member but is supernumerary on board.

As to large individual aid project, these are not exempted and thus should be notified, if aid granted to one firm for a single project exceeds € 1m.

4. Cumulation

The above ceilings apply to national aid and EU co-financed projects and aid shall not be cumulated with other aid for the same eligible costs in case the Regulation ceilings are exceeded.

5. Reporting obligations of Member States

Finally, the Regulation imposes reporting obligations on Member States. Aid exempted by the Regulation shall be compatible provided aid schemes and individual awards express reference to Regulation 68/2001. On implementation of aid, Member States are to provide within 20 working days a summary of the relevant information to the Commission, using the form laid down in Annex II of the Regulation. Member States shall maintain detailed records of all aid for a period of 10 years and, on written request, provide the Commission within 20 workings days all information it considers necessary to assess whether conditions of the Regulation are being complied with. Finally, Member States are required to submit an annual report to the Commission on the application of the Regulation, using the form laid down in Annex III of the Regulation.

6. Example of cumulation

Combining state aid with money from the European Social Fund

Source of Funds	Classification of funds	Recipient of Funds
Case I *Ministry of Labour* **ESF** Company contributions	*National funds: no state aid* **EC funds: no state aid**	Entity that trains unemployed persons in the framework of social security
Case II *Ministry of Labour* **ESF** Company contributions	*National funds: state aid* **EC funds: no state aid** Public funds that have to be cumulated	Firms that train their workers

APPENDIX V
De minimis Aid: Regulation 69/2001

1. Scope

Small amounts of state aid to an undertaking over a given period does not affect trade between Member States and are therefore not caught by Article 87(1) EC.[212] Regulation 69/2001 places a threshold of € 100,000 per undertaking over a period of three years.

The Regulation applies to aid granted in all sectors except that of transport. Further, aid directly linked to export-related activities as well as aid contingent upon the use of domestic over imported goods is not covered by the Regulation.

The Commission has recently adopted a regulation that aid up to € 3,000 per farmer to be considered as *de minimis* in agriculture and fisheries.[213] Furthermore, in these two sectors there is an overall ceiling per Member State.

For the purposes of transparency, equal treatment and correct application of the *de minimis* ceiling, Member States are required to convert aid that is not in the form of a cash grant into its gross cash grant equivalent to establish the amount of aid. When granting *de minimis* aid, Member States are required to inform recipients of the *de minimis* character and obtain full information about other *de minimis* aid received by recipient during the previous three years. In this manner, Member States can check whether the new aid exceeds the *de minimis* ceiling. Further, Member States are required to maintain records for 10 years including all information regarding the application of the Regulation and must provide the Commission with all necessary information, within 20 days, after receiving a written request.

Application of the Regulation is limited to 5 years and thus expires on 31 December 2006. Should the Regulation not be extended, Member States have an adjustment period of 6 months for schemes falling under the Regulation.

2. Cases on cumulation of *de minimis* aid

Commission Decision of 21 January 2003 on the aid scheme 'Stamp duty exemption for non-residential properties in disadvantaged areas' notified by the United Kingdom.[214]

---

212 Case C-351/98, *Spain v Commission*, 2002 ECR I-8031, at para. 51.

213 OJ L325, 28/10/2004. New rules for *de minimis* aid to transport sector are expected in the beginning of 2005.

The scheme would encourage business establishment and property development of a maximum of 2000 areas. The estimated average aid per transaction would be around € 78.500. The scheme could in principle be limited to the field of *de minimis* aid but should beneficiaries be engaged in several property transactions, it would be possible that they might receive more aid than allowed under the *de minimis* Regulation.

The scheme was approved pursuant to Article 87(3)(c) EC.

In *the Netherlands v Commission* the applicants sought to annul Commission Decision 1999/705/EC of 20 July 1999[215] on state aid granted to petrol stations near the German border to offset increase of Dutch taxation in petrol.[216]

The Commission was concerned that the scheme would allow the large oil companies to profit indirectly from the aid granted to small companies linked to them. This is because some oil large companies had agreements with a number of distributors to bear part of the cost of discounts offered by the distributors in response to competition. The aid would release them from that obligation.

That said, the following risks of cumulation of aid were identified:

- in as much as the scheme provides for aid to be granted per service station, the owner of several service stations could by definition receive as many grants of aid as he owns service stations, and
- where an oil company owns one or more service stations, whose freedom is limited by exclusive agreements, that oil company may benefit indirectly from the aid.

The ECJ upheld the Commission's Decision that the *de minimis* rules apply also to indirect aid.

---

[214] OJ L149, 17/06/2003.

[215] OJ L280, 20/07/1999.

[216] Case C-382/1999, 2002 ECR I-5163.

APPENDIX VI
Aid for Small and Medium-Sized Enterprises (SMEs): Regulation 70/2001

1. Introduction

As the Commission points out in recital 5 of the Regulation, SMEs are considered to play a decisive role in job creation and act as a factor of social and economic drive. However, SMEs often have difficulty in obtaining capital or credit whilst their limited resources may restrict access to information notably regarding new technology and potential markets. Considering that SME development may be limited by such market imperfections, the purpose of the aid exempted by Regulation 70/2001 is to facilitate the development of economic activities of SMEs, provided that such aid does not adversely affect trading conditions to the extend contrary to common interest.

The Regulation thus applies to SMEs in all sectors except those of agriculture, fisheries and aquaculture, and is not applicable to any export-related activities or activities where aid is contingent on the use of domestic products. The Regulation is in force for five years thus aid should not be extended beyond December 2006.

2. Definition of an SME

Commission Recommendation of 6 May 2003[217] provides a new definition which has been used since 1 January 2005. This new definition confirms that the number of employees or headcount (includes employees, partners and owners-managers but excludes apprentices) is the main criterion and also for the first time defines the Micro enterprise.

Details are provided in the following table:

Category	Thresholds		
	Employees (main criterion)	Turnover	Balance Sheet
Medium	250	50 mn (1996: 40 mn)	43 mn (1996: 27mn)
Small	50	10 mn (1996: 7 mn)	10 mn (1996: 5mn)

[217] OJ L124, 20/05/2003.

Category	Thresholds		
	Employees (main criterion)	Turnover	Balance Sheet
Micro	10	2 mn	2 mn

To gain a better understanding of the real economic position of SMEs and to remove from that category groups of enterprises whose economic power may exceed that of genuine SMEs, a distinction is made in the new definition between various types of enterprises (see steps below), depending on whether they are autonomous, whether they have holdings which do not entail a controlling position (partner enterprises), or whether they are linked to other enterprises (exercise of control via voting shares, appointment of directors etc.). A limit of a 25% holding below which an enterprise is considered autonomous, is maintained. This threshold can however, be exceeded where the enterprise is held by institutional investors, investment funds, venture capitalists or business "angels," as well as universities or non-profit research centres. If the enterprise is held by autonomous local authorities with less than 5000 people and a budget of less that 10mn it may also be considered an SME, otherwise firms owned by more than 25% by the state are not SMEs.

Steps 1: Autonomous enterprise

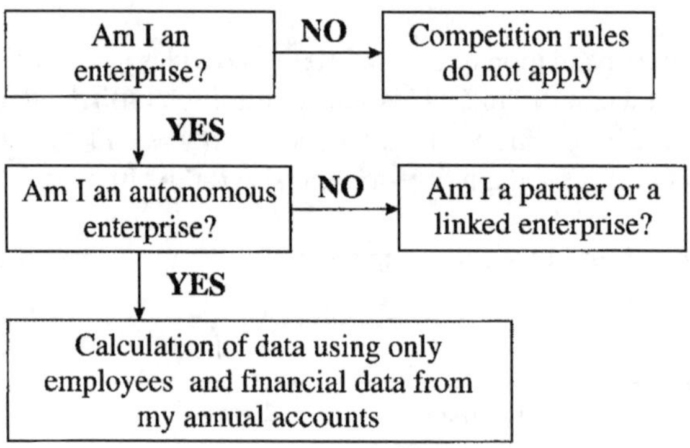

Step 2: Partner enterprise

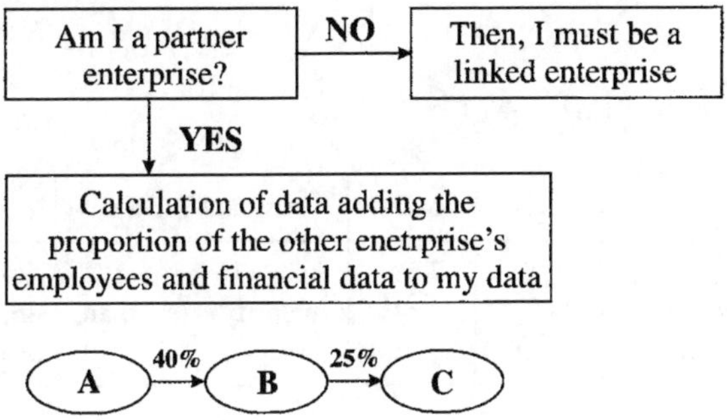

My total is: 100% of B + 40% of A + 25% of C

Step 3: Linked enterprise

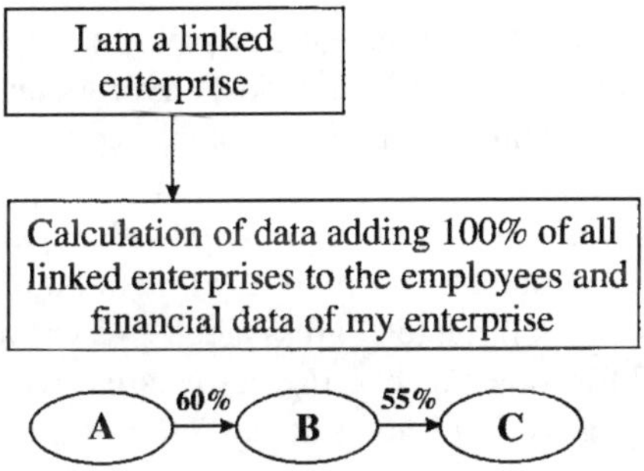

My total is: 100% of B + 100% of A + 100% of C

3. Permissible aid

Permissible aid for SMEs, that is, aid considered compatible with the common market within the meaning of Article 87(3) of the Treaty and exempt from the notification requirement of Article 88(3), is individual aid outside any scheme or aid scheme for:

- **Tangible Investments:** Fixed physical assets in relation to the creation of an establishment, or extension of an existing establishment, or engagement in activity involving fundamental product or production process change.
- **Intangible Investments:** Investment in transfer of technology by the acquisition of patent rights, licenses, know-how or unpatented technical knowledge.
- **Job Creation:** Linked to investments where the jobs are created within 3 years of the investment's completion and are maintained for a minimum period of 5 years.
- **Consultancy and other services and activities:** For services provided by outside

consultants which shall not be a continuous or periodic activity, nor relate to the enterprise's usual operating expenditure and for participation in fair and exhibitions.

4. Permitted intensities

	SEs	MEs	Article 87 (3)(a)	Article 87 (3)(c)
Investment (Gross aid as percentage of eligible cost)	15%	7.5%	Ram +15% if net intensity is less than 75%	Ram +10% if net intensity is less than 30%

- These higher regional allowances only apply if the investment is maintained for a minimum period of 5 years and the recipient contributes 25% to its financing.
- Eligible costs: for tangible assets shall be the costs relating to investment in land, buildings, machinery and equipment but not transport means and equipment. For intangible assets shall be the costs of the acquisition of the technology.

In the cases where aid is calculated on the basis of jobs created, the amount of aid shall be expressed as a percentage of the wage costs over a period of two years. Finally, for services and fairs/exhibitions, aid may not exceed 50% of fees and first-time exhibition costs.

Article 6 of the Regulation places a limit on large individual grants which it shall exempt. Thus, individual grants must be notified if (a) the total eligible cost of the project is greater than 25mn, or (b) if the total gross aid is greater than 15mn. In addition, notification is required for projects covering firstly, areas which do not qualify for regional aid and where the gross intensity is at least 50% of the 7.5% or 15% ceilings discussed above and secondly, projects in assisted areas, where the net aid intensity is at least 50% of the net aid ceiling as determined in the regional aid map for the area concerned.

The aid ceilings discussed above shall apply regardless of whether the support is financed entirely from state resources or is partly financed by the community. Aid exempted by this Regulation, cannot be cumulated with any other state aid within the meaning of Article 87(1) of the Treaty, or with any other Community funding, if such cumulation would result in aid intensity exceeding the Regulation ceilings.

5. Reporting obligations of Member States

Finally, the Regulation imposes reporting obligations on Member States. Aid exempted by the Regulation shall be compatible provided aid schemes and individual awards express reference to Regulation 70/2001. On implementation of aid, Member States are to provide within 20 working days a summary of the relevant information to the Commission, using the form laid down in Annex II of the Regulation. Member States shall maintain detailed records of all aid for a period of 10 years and, on written request, provide the Commission within 20 workings days all information it considers necessary to assess whether conditions of the Regulation are being complied with. Finally, Member States are required to submit an annual report to the Commission on the application of the Regulation, using the form laid down in Annex III of the Regulation.

6. Revised Regulation including R&D (Regulation 364/2004 of 25 February 2004)

This Regulation applies the same principles and definitions of the stages of R&D as in the R&D Framework (see Appendix IX)

	SMEs	Article 87 (3)(a)	Article 87 (3)(c)	Multisectoral application or in 6th FRM	Cross-border cooperation/ cooperation with public research body/ widely disseminated results
Fundamental research (Gross aid as percentage of eligible cost)	100%				
Industrial research (Gross aid as percentage of eligible cost)	60%	+10%	+5%	+15%	+10%
Pre-competitive development (Gross aid as percentage of eligible cost)	35%	+10%	+5%	+15%	+10%

Overall ceiling: 75% for industrial and 50% for pre-competitive development.

Technical feasibility studies for industrial research or pre-competitive developments activities are eligible for aid under Article 87(3)(c) EC, provided that the gross aid intensity, as calculated on the basis of study costs, does not exceed 75%. Also, aid for patenting costs should be up to the same level of aid as that received by the research that led to the patents concerned.

APPENDIX VII
Employment Aid: Regulation 2204/2002

1. Introduction

The Regulation is in force since January 2003 and will be valid until 31 December 2006. It applies to aid schemes, which provide aid for the creation of employment, the recruitment of disadvantaged and disabled workers or in order to cover the additional costs of employing disabled workers. General measures however are not covered under this Regulation. Such measures may be: lower taxation of labour and lower employer contributions, investment in education and training, provision of guidance and counselling, assistance and training for the unemployed and improvement in labour law.

The Regulation thus applies to aid in all sectors including those of agriculture, fisheries and aquaculture, and is not applicable to aid granted in the coal or shipbuilding sectors nor to aid granted for the creation of employment in the transport sector. It also excludes any aid to export-related activities or activities where aid is contingent on the use of domestic products.

2. Definitions

Disadvantaged worker: any person with difficulties entering the labour market without assistance:

- Person under 25, not in previous employment
- Migrant worker
- Ethnic minority worker requiring development of its work experience
- Person who re-enters working life
- Person living alone, looking after a child
- Person with no secondary qualification or no job
- Person older that 50 with no job or losing his/her job
- Long-term unemployed person (12 months)
- Addicts or person imprisoned before first job
- Any woman in NUTS II areas and where female unemployment has exceeded 150% of the male unemployment rate

Disabled worker: person recognised by national law to have serious disabilities.

3. Permissible aid

Aid schemes fulfilling the conditions of the Regulation are considered compatible and thus exempted from the notification requirement of Article 88(3) EC, if they contain an express reference to this Regulation.

However, Member States may still notify aid in some circumstances:

- when targeted at particular sectors where special guidelines exist, e.g. rescue & restructuring, multisectoral framework
- when granted to single firm exceeding € 15m gross over 3 years
- to maintain jobs only if it remedies damage by natural disaster or exceptional occurrence or under the rules in operating aid in the 87(3)(a) areas
- to convert temporary or fixed-term contracts
- for job-sharing schemes
- to encourage early retirement.

4. Permitted intensities

	SEs	MEs	Article 87(3)(a)	Article 87(3)(c)
Creation of employment (Gross aid as percentage of wage cost)	15%	7.5%	+15% if net intensity is less than 75%	+10% if net intensity is less than 30%

The higher regional allowances only apply if the employment is maintained within the qualifying region and the recipient contributes 25% to its financing.

The Regulation applies for aid measures according to which the employment created represents a net increase of employees compared with the average over past 12 months and it is maintained for a minimum period of 3 years or 2 years in the case of SMEs. New workers employed as a result of employment must have never had a job or have lost their previous job. For exemption under this Regulation, the application must be submitted before recruitment or investment takes place and the employment is created within 3 years of investment completion.

	Disadvantaged workers	Disabled workers
Recruitment of D&D workers (Gross aid as percentage of wage cost over a period of one year)	50%	60%

	Disadvantaged workers	Disabled workers
Aid for additional costs		• Reduced productivity • Costs of adapting premises and equipment • Costs of employing staff for time spent to assist the workers

5. Cumulation

The aid ceilings discussed above shall apply regardless of whether the support is financed entirely from state resources or is partly financed by the community. Aid exempted by this Regulation, cannot be cumulated with any other state aid within the meaning of Article 87(1) of the Treaty, or with any other Community funding, if such cumulation would result in aid intensity exceeding the Regulation ceilings.

Cumulation is allowed however in cases of D&D worker, if aid is less than 100% of the wage costs.

6. Reporting obligations of Member States

Finally, the Regulation imposes reporting obligations on Member States. On implementation of aid, Member States are to provide within 20 working days a summary of the relevant information to the Commission, using the form laid down in Annex I of the Regulation. Member States shall maintain detailed records of all aid for a period of 10 years and, on written request, provide the Commission within 20 workings days all information it considers necessary to assess whether conditions of the Regulation are being complied with. Finally, Member States are required to submit an annual report to the Commission on the application of the Regulation, using the form laid down in Annex II of the Regulation.

APPENDIX VIII
Aid for Rescue and Restructuring of Companies in Difficulty

1. Introduction

One of the most vexed issues in economic policy is whether the government should rescue companies that find themselves in financial trouble. The problems at the French company Alstom and more recently the scandal at the Italian company Parmalat, both of which are prominent European companies in their fields, demonstrate how difficult it is for any government to resist calls to provide liquidity to avert the demise of a large company. A function of the European Community is indeed to protect governments from domestic pressure to subsidise whichever company happens to have lobbying power.

However, state aid may be justified in some situations where markets do not function properly or when the failure of a company would have damaging effects on the economy. Because a blanket prohibition of state aid would prevent national authorities from intervening when such intervention would be justified by economic or other considerations, the EC system for control of state aid has guidelines and frameworks that lay down specific rules on the kind and amount of state aid that may be granted by national authorities. These rules also include guidelines on state aid for rescuing and restructuring companies.

2. Commission concerns

In the 2003 Autumn edition[218] of the state aid Scoreboard, the Commission made for the first time public its views on the issues it thought problematic in relation to rescue and restructuring aid. According to the Commission, "a first internal review of the guidelines has identified a series of problems, a selection of which are presented below:"

"i. **When is a company in financial difficulties?** There is no Community definition of a "firm in difficulty" and it seems very difficult to derive any definition from the practice of member states because of differences in national insolvency laws and procedures."[219]

"ii. **Groups of companies**. The guidelines state that a company belonging to a group is not normally eligible, except where the difficulties are the com-

[218] European Commission, State Aid Scoreboard, COM(2003) 636 final, 29/10/2003.

pany's own and are not the result of an arbitrary allocation of costs within the group, while the difficulties are too serious to be dealt with by the group itself. These criteria are not easily applicable and raise a number of questions. For example, where a subsidiary in one member state is in financial difficulties but whose parent company appears unwilling to support it."

"**iii. Urgency**. Whereas the current guidelines are based on the premise that aid is notified in advance, rescue aid often has to be granted prior to Commission approval in order to avoid the collapse of the company. However, any possible solution to this situation should comply with the notification obligation under Art. 88 (3) EC Treaty."

"**iv. One-time last time principle**. The guidelines provide that rescue aid is a one-off operation and that repeated rescue aids should be avoided. However, there have been cases of companies which were not eligible for restructuring aid because of the "one time, last time" principle, obtaining new rescue aid."

"**v. Various time limits**. The different time limits in the current framework are unclear and thus need to be clarified."

"**vi. Compensatory measures**. When are the compensatory measures proposed sufficient in scope "to mitigate the potentially distortive effects of the aid on competition"?"[220]

The six issues identified by the Commission relate largely to the clarity of the various definitions and the ease of application of key concepts. In addition, the Commission grapples with a substantive problem – the extent of compensatory measures.

3. The main features of the guidelines on rescue and restructuring

The current guidelines, which were in principle adopted by the European Commission on 7 July 2004, replace the 1999 guidelines and apply to all aid notified after 10 October 2004. They are due to expire in October 2009.[221] The current guidelines are applicable to all sectors except motor vehicles, air transport and shipbuilding. Special provisions exist for agricultural products.[222]

In this context, under the 1999 guidelines state aid may be granted for two purposes: rescuing and/or restructuring. Aid for rescuing should normally be in the form of a short-term loan (normally not longer than six months) or loan guarantee at mar-

---

219 For an account of these problems see E. Valle and K. van de Casteele, *"Revision of the Rescue and Restructuring Guidelines: A Crackdown?"*, 1-European State Aid Law Quarterly, 2004, p. 9.

220 State Aid Scoreboard, p. 28.

221 Community Guidelines on State Aid for Rescuing and Restructuring Firms in Difficulty, OJ C244, 01/10/2004. See "http://europa.eu.int/eur-lex/pri/en/oj/dat/1999/c_288/c_28819991009en00020018.pdf".

222 For a more detailed analysis of the provisions of the guidelines see P. Anestis, S. Mavroghenis and S. Drakakakis, *"Rescue and Restructuring Aid"*, 1 – European State Aid Law Quarterly, 2004, p. 27.

ket rates of interest. The intention is that within that period the firm that receives the rescue aid should put in place a plan for restructuring that would bring it back to financial viability in the medium term (approximately in a five- years period). The original rescue loan has to be repaid within twelve months.

Aid for restructuring may take various forms but it is usually either a long-term loan or an injection of new share capital. Some times aid is granted in the form of tax or social security relief or loan write-off.

Since rescue or restructuring aid undermines the discipline of the market, one may justifiably wonder why the EC allows such aid. The Commission itself acknowledges that "(a)id for rescue and restructuring firms in difficulty is undoubtedly one of the most potentially distortive types of state aid. It cannot be the norm that a company which runs into difficulties is kept artificially in the market by the state. The exit of unprofitable firms is a normal part of the functioning of a market economy."[223]

The guidelines provide three reasons why aid may be allowed. According to the guidelines "(t)he provision of rescue or restructuring aid to firms in difficulty may only be regarded as legitimate subject to certain conditions. It may be justified, for instance, by social or regional policy considerations, by the need to take into account the beneficial role played by small and medium-sized enterprises (SMEs) in the economy or, exceptionally, by the desirability of maintaining a competitive market structure when the demise of firms could lead to a monopoly or to a tight oligopolistic situation".[224]

Towards meeting these three objectives, the Commission authorises restructuring aid only if the following conditions are all satisfied:

i. **A realistic restructuring plan is put in place.** The plan must identify the causes of the company's difficulties and formulate measures to address those difficulties under reasonable assumptions concerning both internal changes that the company is capable of implementing (e.g. reorganisation and rationalisation) and expected external changes in market conditions (e.g. exit from activities and projects that will continue suffering losses).
ii. **Restoration of financial and commercial viability.** The restructuring plan must be capable of bringing the company to viability in the sense that its expected revenue should be sufficient to cover its financial outlays and operating costs and generate an acceptable return to its shareholders.
iii. **State aid must be kept at a minimum.** The beneficiary company should not receive more aid than is strictly necessary to implement its restructuring plan. At the same time, the shareholders of the beneficiary company should make a substantial contribution of their own money. The company may not use the aid to expand its activities or undertake investments, which are unrelated to restructuring. Nor, may it use state aid to acquire other companies.
iv. **No undue distortion of competition.** The company should compensate its competitors for the aid it receives. In sectors with over-capacity, the Commission nor-

---

[223] European Commission, State Aid Scoreboard, COM(2003) 636 final, 29/10/2003, p. 13.
[224] Paragraph 8, at p.3.

mally requires that the beneficiary company closes down capacity or sells assets to competitors or gives up market share (e.g. landing slots). The company may also not be allowed to act as price leader or sell below cost. These restrictions are waived when the beneficiary is an SME or when it has a "negligible" market share. When the recipient is located in an assisted area, the extent of compensatory measures (e.g. reduction of capacity) that is requested by the Commission is correspondingly lower.

v. **Aid is authorised "one time, last time."** In principle, this means that companies cannot be rescued or restructured repeatedly. Otherwise the discipline of the market is removed. In practice, however, "one time, last time" means not more than once per ten years.

4. A comparison of the old and new guidelines

The new guidelines retain many of the provisions of the old guidelines. They retain the definition of undertakings in difficulty, the case of groups of companies, the principles that restructuring aid must be the minimum necessary, that it should be accompanied by a plan to restore the recipient firm to viability within a reasonable length of time, that it should not cause undue distortion to competition and that restructuring aid may not be granted more than once (at least, not more than once every ten-year period). Some of the Commission's concerns thus, as above mentioned, have not been satisfied in the new guidelines.

The main differences between the two sets of guidelines are as follows:

i. **Rescue aid.** The concept of rescue aid has been widened. Rescue aid that is granted for at most six months and has to be repaid by the end of the six-month period, otherwise it will be counted in the overall amount of restructuring aid.

ii. **Simplified procedure.** A major innovation of the new guidelines is that rescue aid is assessed through a simplified and expedited assessment process. In addition, rescue aid is subject to "the one-time, last-time" principle.

iii. **Maximum amount of rescue aid.** The maximum amount of rescue aid to qualify for the simplified procedure is determined on the basis of a formula, which is defined in an annex to the new guidelines.

iv. **SMEs.** No restructuring plan is required to be submitted in the case of SMEs. The grant of aid must however be conditional on full implementation of a restructuring plan, which is communicated to the Commission and has been approved by the member state concerned.

v. **Compensatory measures.** The compensatory measures may have to be as high as 100% of the beneficiary company's capacity in case that the beneficiary operates in a market with long-term structural problems. Also, the new guidelines have dropped the reference to "negligible" market share but compensatory measures are now in principle also required from medium-sized enterprises.

vi. **Own contribution.** The money that has to be contributed by the shareholders of the beneficiary company must be at least 25% for small enterprises, 40% for medium-sized enterprises and 50% for large enterprises.

APPENDIX IX
Aid for Research & Development

1. Introduction

Article 157(1) EC states that the Community and Member States shall aim at "fostering better exploitation of the industrial potential of policies of innovation, research and technological development". Further, Article 157(3) EC stipulates that the Community is to contribute to the achievement of this objective "through the policies and activities it pursues under other provisions of this Treaty". To this end, the Community Framework for state aid for Research and Development[225] aims at implementing competition rules effectively whilst contributing towards this objective.

The Commission has in general adopted a favourable attitude towards state aid for R&D. This is due to the fact that R&D is seen as playing a beneficial role and contributes towards renewing growth, strengthening competitiveness and boosting employment. Further, companies may be reluctant to invest in R&D due to the considerable risks involved and thus require an incentive. Given the distance from the marketplace of R&D operations, the likelihood that such aid will distort competition and trade is reduced. The framework thus aims to minimise distortions and maximise the incentive effect created by such aid.

Note that in May 2002 the framework was extended to 31 December 2005 with no changes, whilst a new Regulation 364/2004 on R&D in SMEs came into force on 25 February 2004 (see Appendix VI).

2. Categories of R&D

The closer the R&D operation is to the market, the more significant may be the distortive effect of the state aid. In order to determine the proximity to the market of the aided R&D, the Commission makes a distinction between fundamental research, industrial research and pre-competitive development activities. These are defines as follows:

- **Fundamental Research:** "activity designed to broaden scientific and technical knowledge not linked to industrial or commercial objective". It thus presupposes wide dissemination of the results.
- **Industrial Research:** "planned research of critical investigation aimed at the acquisition of new knowledge, the objective being that such knowledge may be

[225] OJ C45, 17/02/1996.

useful in developing new products, processes or services or in bringing about significant improvement in existing products, processes or services", e.g. project within EUREKA.[226]

- **Pre-competitive Development Activity:** "the shaping of the results of industrial research into a plan, arrangement of design for new, altered or improved products, processes or services, whether they are intended to be sold or used", e.g. the Dutch aid to Hoogovens Staal for Cyclone Converter Furnace (CFF) for direct production of liquid iron.[227]

3. Compatibility of aid for R&D

Public financing of R&D by public non-profit higher education or research establishments is not considered as aid, provided that the results are available Community-wide and on a non-discriminatory basis. If such R&D occurs in collaboration with industry the Commission will not consider it aid if services are rendered on a commercial basis or industry bears the full market cost. Public authorities may commission or buy the results from R&D directly from firms provided such contracts are awarded according to market conditions.

The Framework provides two possibilities for exemptions. Under Article 87(3)(b), state aid for R&D will be considered compatible if the purpose of the aid is to promote an important project of common European interest. The common interest must be demonstrable in practical terms. Secondly, Article 87(3)(c) may enable compatibility for aid that facilitates certain economic activities as long as it does not adversely effect trading conditions to an extent contrary to common interest.

4. Permitted Intensities

Permitted intensities for aid for R&D is determined on a case-by-case basis and is assessed by the Commission in light of the projects assessed distance from the market; the nature of the project; the competitiveness of the European industry; the risk of distortion to competition and the effect on trade between Member States.

	Fundamental research	Industrial research	Precompetitive dev. activities
Standard limits	100%	50%	25%
SMEs		+10%	+10%
Art.87(3)(a) region		+10%	+10%
Art. 87(3)(c) region		+5%	+5%

226 *Individual cases under the MEDEA+ scheme*, Case N 702/B/2001, OJ C 292, 27/11/2002.
227 IP/98/284

	Fundamental research	Industrial research	Precompetitive dev. activities
Part of R&D Community framework		+15%	+15%
Projects with cross-border cooperation		+10%	+10%
Projects with cooperation between firms and public research bodies		+10%	+10%
Results widely disseminated		+10%	+10%
Preparatory technical feasibility studies		75%	50%
Maximum ceilings		75%	50%

Eligible costs include: personnel costs, costs of instruments, equipment, land and premises, cost of consultancy, additional overheads, other operating expenses linked to the research activity, special tools used exclusively for R&D that may not be used in manufacturing.

5. Incentive effect of R&D aid

State aid for R&D should serve as an incentive for firms to undertake R&D activities in addition to their normal day-to-day operations. It may also encourage firms not carrying out R&D to undertake such activities. Where this incentive effect is not evident, the Commission may consider such aid less favourably than it usually does. The incentive effect is assumed to exist in case of SMEs.

In order to verify that the planned aid will induce firms to pursue research which they would not have normally pursued, the Commission will take into account quantifiable factors such as net increase in R&D expenditure; staff increases in R&D related activities and so forth. In addition, it will account for market failures and the additional costs related to cross-border co-operation, as well as other relevant factors indicated by the Member State. If no incentive effect is demonstrated, the R&D aid is considered to be an operating aid and will be prohibited.[228]

6. Reporting obligations of Member States

State aid for R&D has to be notified to the Commission by means of the standard form sent out to Member States dated 22 February 1994. The supplementary questionnaire on R&D found in Annex III of the framework should be included. To

[228] IP/01/784.

achieve the highest possible transparency, the Commission requires a clear statement of objectives, beneficiaries etc. The different categories of costs, which the aid is designed to reduce must be specified and the aid must be granted in such a form that the intensity of the aid in relation to these costs (as listed in Annex II of the framework) can be calculated. Should the aid not be paid in the form of a outright grant, Member States are required to ensure that the Commission is able to calculate the grant equivalent of the aid, and thus must supply enough information to do so.

Individual grants of aid under a R&D scheme that has been authorised by the Commission do not need to be notified, however prior notification is required of any individual research project costing more than ECU 25 million and for which it is proposed to provide aid with a gross grant equivalent of more than ECU 5 million. Finally, for each authorised aid scheme, the Commission will generally request an annual report on the implementation and so be in a position to monitor the allocation of aid, and if necessary, propose appropriate measures if it considers that the scheme is distorting.

APPENDIX X
Aid for Environmental Protection

1. General Principles

The purpose of these guidelines is to ensure whether, and under what conditions, aid may be regarded as necessary to ensure environmental protection and sustainable development without having disproportionate effects on competition and economic growth. They apply to all sectors excluding the field covered by the Community guidelines for state aid in the agricultural sector. They also do not cover environmental aid to R&D and training, as the R&D framework and the Regulation on training aid respectively cover these aids, and stranded costs, which are dealt with separately. Further, measures that serve a public service obligation do not fall under these guidelines, especially borderline cases, such as waste treatment, water supply etc. The guidelines are valid until 31 December 2007.

2. Definitions

- **Environmental protection:** any action to remedy or prevent damage to physical surroundings or natural resources, or to encourage efficient use of resources (e.g. energy-saving measures, use of renewable sources of energy).
- **"Polluter pays" principle:** the costs of measures to reduce pollution should be borne by polluter who causes pollution.
- **Internalisation of costs:** all costs associated with protection of environment should be included in firms' production costs.
- **Community standard:** setting the levels to be attained in environmental terms and the obligation under Community law to use the best available techniques with no excessive costs.
- **Renewable energy sources:** non-fossil energy sources, viz. wind energy, solar energy, geothermal energy, wave energy, tidal energy etc.
- **Eligible costs:** are those limited to the extra costs necessary to meet the environmental objectives. Costs designed to bring companies into line with standards are not eligible, with the exception of SMEs for a 3-year period since the adoption of the standards. The eligible costs must be calculated net of the benefits.

3. Permissible aid

Investment aid	Basic rates
To adapt to new Community standards	0*
To improve on or in the absence of Community standards	30
In energy saving	40
In combined production of electricity power and heat	40
To promote renewable sources of energy	40
In renewable energy installations for an entire community	50
To support renewable energy when shown to be necessary	100
To rehabilitate a polluted industrial site	100 + 15**
To relocate firms	30

* SMEs: 15% (maximum of 3 years).

** up to 100% of the eligible costs (= cost of the work – increase in the value of the land) plus 15% of the cost of the work.

- Bonus for SMEs: +10 percentage points
- Bonus for assisted regions: higher of either +5% in 87(3)(c), +10% in 87(3)(a) or regional ceiling + 10% (but no double bonus for SMEs).

<table>
<tr><th>Operating aid</th><th>General rules</th></tr>
<tr><td>To promote waste management and energy savings</td><td rowspan="5">• 5 years duration
• up to 100% for degressive aid but has to fall linearly to 0% by the end of the 5th year
• up to 50% of the extra costs for non-degressive aid</td></tr>
<tr><td>Tax reductions or exemptions</td></tr>
<tr><td>For renewable energy sources (4options)</td></tr>
<tr><td>For the combined production of electric power and heat</td></tr>
<tr><td>To encourage the development of processes for producing electric power from conventional energy sources but with higher energy efficiency</td></tr>
</table>

Operating aid, cont.

Tax Reductions or Exemptions	• Autonomous MS decision => compatible (temporarily) • EC decision: – national rate ≥ minimum EC rate => compatible – national rate < minimum EC rate - if not allowed by EC directive => incompatible - if allowed by EC directive => compatible if it is necessary, proportional, strictly limited in time
	Ceilings If MS introduces new tax or if EC rate is lower • reduction without degressivity for 10 years if: – agreement between MS and firms on efficiency targets with the possibility of sanctions e.g. climate-change levy exemption for some UK industries, with commitment to reduce pollution emission over time • non-conditional on agreement if: – national tax rate paid by firms is higher than EC rate – or, in the absence of EC std, firm pays significant proportion of national tax In other cases: max 5 years (i.e. 100% → 0% degressively or 50% flat)
Renewable energy sources	*Four options:* • To cover the difference in production costs and market price • Market mechanism (e.g. green certificates) • Aid calculated on basis of avoidable external costs (never used) • General rules for operating aid (as above)

APPENDIX XI
Aid in the Agricultural Sector: Community Guidelines and Regulation 1/2004

1. General principles

The guidelines for state aid in the agricultural sector apply to all sectors excluding fisheries, aquaculture and forestry.[229] Also, the Commission's guidelines on regional aid as well as the Regulation 70/2001 on aid to SMEs and Regulation 69/2001 on *de minimis* aid are not applicable in the agricultural sector.[230] The competition rules apply to the agricultural sector only to the extent determined by the Council and are subject to any restrictions, which may have been laid down by the Council in the regulations establishing the common market organisations CMO.

Therefore, Article 87 and 88 EC apply to state aid granted to the agricultural sector with the exception of aid for the production of and trade in products that are not covered by a CMO. In addition, the Commission can under no circumstance approve aid, which is contrary to a CMO or which would interfere with the proper functioning of the CMO.

For aid targeted to products not covered by a CMO, such as aid for potatoes other than starch potatoes, horsemeat, honey, coffee, alcohol of agricultural origin and vinegars derived from alcohol and cork, the Commission, following Council Regulation 26/1962 applying certain rules of competition to production of and trade in agricultural products,[231] cannot oppose the granting of such aids, although it may submit its comments.

The guidelines clarify what is not explicitly fixed by regulations. In order for aid to be considered compatible with the common market, the following principles apply, unless exceptions are expressly provided by EC law:

- aid must have incentive element
- operating aid is considered to be incompatible with the common market
- retrospectively granted aid does not have incentive element
- application for aid must be submitted before work is started
- aid must not infringe Article 6 EC on environmental protection and all notifications must contain an environmental impact assessment

---

[229] State aid in the fisheries and aquaculture sector are examined within the framework of specific Guidelines (OJ C229, 14/09/2004) and Regulation 2468/98 (OJ L312, 20/11/1998).

[230] The Commission has adopted a regulation concerning *de minimis* aid in the agriculture sector, according to which aid up to € 3000 per farmer and fisherman over three years from the requirement of prior notification is exempted (OJ L325, 28/10/2004).

[231] OJ 30, 20/04/1962.

2. Permissible aid

Investment aid

In agricultural holdings:

Objectives	Aid intensity (expressed as percentage of eligible investment)
• Reduce production costs • Improve production • Increase quality • Improve environment	40% or 50% in less favoured areas increased by 5% in case of young farmers

Eligible costs: the construction, acquisition or improvement of immovable property, new machinery and equipment, general costs such as architects, engineers etc., land purchase.

Special cases	Aid intensity
Conservation of traditional landscapes	100% of real costs incurred for non-productive heritage features 60% or 75% in the less favoured areas of the eligible expenses for heritage features of productive assets
Relocation of farm buildings in the public interest	100% of the actual costs
Protection and improvement of environment and hygiene	60% or 75% of eligible investment in less favoured areas

Processing and marketing of agricultural products
Eligible costs: same as agricultural holdings above.
Permissible aid: 40% or 50% of eligible investments in less favoured areas

Promoting the diversification of farm activities
They fall within the scope of the Rural Development Regulation. The Commission however takes a favourable view of such aid, which it considers likely to favour the development of the rural economy as a whole.

Environmental aid

For environmental investments
Same as above under investment aid.

For agri-environmental commitments
Aid is calculated in terms of income foregone and additional costs, whereas the rate for permissible aid should not exceed 20% of the of income foregone and additional costs.

For farmers in areas with environmental restrictions
Aid to compensate for costs incurred and income foregone resulting from environmental restrictions. The maximum amount of aid is fixed at € 200/ha, whereas the total surface of these areas should not exceed 10% of the surface area of the Member State concerned.

Operating aid
Aid must clearly offset the additional costs arising from the use new mandatory national environmental requirements. It must be both temporary and degressive, in principle over no more than 5 years, and the initial amount of aid should not exceed the amount necessary to compensate the producer for the additional cost of compliance with the relevant national requirements.

Aid to compensate for handicaps in the less-favoured areas

Social aid

Permissible aid up to € 25,000 for the setting up of young farmers and up to 100% for early retirement.

Aid for closing down production

Aid limited to compensation of loss of value of assets plus incentive payment, which may not exceed 20% of the value of assets.

Aid for producer group

Aid must be temporary and degressive and must not exceed 100% of eligible costs incurred in the first year. The aid level must be reduced by at least 20% for each year of operation, so that in the 5th year the amount of aid is limited to 20% of actual costs in that year.

Aid to compensate for damage caused

By natural disasters or exceptional occurrences
Earthquakes, avalanches, landslides, floods, war, internal disturbances or strikes and depending on their extent, major nuclear or industrial accidents, fires and very widespread outbreaks of new animal diseases are considered by the Commission to constitute natural disasters or exceptional occurrences under Article 87(2)(b). Permissible aid in those cased may be granted for up to 100% to compensate for material damage.

By adverse weather conditions
Events such as frost, hail, ice, rain or drought may be assimilated to natural disasters once the level of damage reaches a certain threshold, which has been fixed at 20% of normal gross production of the relevant crop in the year in question in the less-favoured areas and 30% in other areas. Notifications should include appropriate supporting meteorological information.

Aid to compensate farmers for damage to buildings and equipment is accepted up to 100% of actual costs, without any minimum threshold being applied.

By animal and plant diseases
Aid to compensate for damage caused by animal and plant diseases may only be permitted on the basis of Article 87(3)(c), as part of an appropriate programme at Community, national or regional level for the prevention, control or eradication of the disease concerned. Such aid may be granted at up to 100% of actual costs incurred.

Aid towards the payment of insurance premiums
Commission allows aid of up to 80% of the cost of insurance premiums to cover against losses caused by natural disasters or exceptional occurrences and adverse weather conditions. The rate is reduced to 50% of the cost of the premium for losses caused by animal or plant diseases.

Aid for land reparcelling

Permissible aid up to 100% of actual costs incurred. If aid for investment is granted within a reparcelling scheme, the rates set out above under investment aid apply respectively.

Aid for production and marketing of quality products

Permissible activities	Rates
• Market research and technical studies • Introduction of quality assurance schemes • Training	• Not more than € 100.000 per company/3 years • 50% of the eligible costs for SMEs • up to 100% for the costs of compulsory quality controls • up to 70% for the costs of non compulsory quality controls • up to 100% of the costs for controls of organic production methods

Routine in-process quality controls and routine product controls are not eligible for aid.

Aid to provide technical support

Permissible aid up to 100% of costs to cover activities such as education and training, farm management and replacement services, consultants' fees etc.

Aid for the livestock sector

In order to support the maintenance and improvement of the genetic quality of Community livestock:

Costs	Aid intensity
Administrative costs of the establishment and maintenance of herd books	100%
For tests to determine the genetic quality or yield of livestock	70%
For investments in animal reproduction centres and for the introduction at farm level of innovatory animal breeding techniques or practices	40%
For keeping individual male breeding animals of high genetic quality registered in herd books	30%

Aid for the outermost regions and the Aegean islands

3. Procedural matters

- All new aid schemes and all new individual aids must be notified to the Commission
- No separate notification is required in respect of aid granted in conjunction with EC support
- Member States are required to submit annual reports on all existing aid schemes

4. Regulation 1/2004 on the application of state aid rules to SMEs in the agricultural sector

4.1 General Principles

This Regulation shall apply to aid granted to SMEs active in the production, processing or marketing of the agricultural products of Annex I to the EC Treaty. It shall not apply to aid covering advertising costs, aid granted to processing of Annex I products into non-Annex I products, aid to individual projects that exceed a fixed maximum amount, export aid or aid contingent upon the use of domestic over imported products. Individual aid and aid schemes that fulfil the conditions of the Regulation shall be exempt for the notification requirement provided that they contain express reference to the Regulation. The latter applies until 31 December 2006.

4.2 Permissible aid

Investment aid

In agricultural holdings:

Objectives	Aid intensity (expressed as percentage of eligible investment)
• Reduce production costs • Improve production • Increase quality • Improve environment • Promote diversification	40% or 50% in less favoured areas increased by 10% in case of young farmers and by 25% and 20% respectively where investments result in extra costs (e.g. environmental protection)

Eligible costs: the construction, acquisition or improvement of immovable property, new machinery and equipment, general costs such as architects, engineers etc., land purchase.

Special Cases	Aid intensity
Conservation of traditional landscapes	As above under 2
Relocation of farm buildings in the public interest	As above under 2
Processing and marketing	As above under 2
Setting up of young farmers	As above under 2
Early retirement	As above under 2
Producer groups	As above under 2, but the total amount of aid < € 100.000
Payment of insurance premiums	As above under 2, but in case for losses caused by adverse climatic events that can be assimilated to natural disasters, loss for 1st year >10% of gross production and the real loss >20% in the less-favoured areas and >30% in other areas.
Land reparcelling	As above under 2

Special Cases	Aid intensity
Production and marketing of quality products	• Not more than € 100.000 per company/3 years • up to 100% for the costs of market research activities • up to 100% for the costs of introducing quality assurance schemes • up to 100% of the costs of training personnel • up to 100% of the costs of the initial certification of quality assurance systems • up to 100% of the costs of compulsory control measures • up to 100% of the costs for controls of organic production methods
Provision of technical support	Total amount must not exceed € 100.000 per beneficiary/3 years or 50% of the eligible costs, for activities such as education and training, farm management and replacement services, consultants' fees exhibition fees etc.
Support for the livestock sector	As above under 2 plus 100% towards the costs of TSE tests

APPENDIX XII
Case Study on Recovery of Aid

(Land Rheinland-Pfalz v Alcan Deutschland GmbH)

Date	Event
7/3/83	Commission gets information ex officio about proposed aid and requests information from Federal Government
9/6/83	Decision of Land R-P (State Authority) granting aid of DM 4 million (out of DM 8 million in total) without prior notification to the Commission
25/7/83	Federal Government confirms intention of State Authority to grant the aid
11/10/83	Commission commences preliminary examination
25/11/83	Commission opens the formal investigation procedure
28/11/83	State Authority is informed of the opening of formal investigation
30/11/83	Decision of State Authority to grant the remaining DM 4 million
13/12/83	Alcan (the beneficiary) is informed that aid has not been notified
14/12/85	Decision 86/60/EEC of the Commission on illegality and incompatibility of the aid measure. It orders the recovery.
15/1/86	The beneficiary is informed of the Commission decision
12/2 and 21/4/86	The Commission is informed by the Federal Government about political and legal obstacles to the recovery of the aid
27/6/86	Commission insists on recovery
Neither the beneficiary nor the Federal Government comply with the Commission decision and the latter refer the case to the ECJ	
2/2/89	ECJ holds that Federal Government failed to comply with the Commission decision
26/9/89	State Authority revokes decisions of 9/6 and 30/11/1983 and asks repayment

<table>
<tr><th>Date</th><th>Event</th></tr>
<tr><td colspan="2">The beneficiary brought an action against the decision of 26/9/89, which succeeded before the Administrative Court. The State Authority appealed to the Higher Administrative Court but its action was dismissed and then it appealed on points of law to the Federal Administrative Court, which made the request for the preliminary ruling of the ECJ. Briefly, the Federal Administrative Court asked whether the State Authority is obliged to revoke a decision granting unlawful aid if: i. the State Authority has allowed the time-limit, which exists for that purpose under national law, in the interest of legal certainty to elapse; ii. the State Authority is responsible for the illegality of the aid decision to such a degree that revocation appears to be a breach of good faith towards the beneficiary; and iii. recovery would be excluded by national law because the gain no longer exists, in the absence of bad faith on the part of the beneficiary.</td></tr>
<tr><td>20/3/97</td><td>Judgement of the ECJ</td></tr>
<tr><td colspan="2">In answering the first question the ECJ said that the beneficiary could not have had a legitimate expectation that the aid was lawful, given that he knew that the aid was given without prior notification and that it was paid without the Commission's prior advice. Besides, as long as the Commission has declared the incompatibility of the measure, which has not been challenged in legal proceedings, the national authorities are simply there to give effect of that decision and have thus no discretion on revocation. With the same token, the beneficiary could not be held as being deprived of legal certainty. As to the second question, the ECJ held that the beneficiary's obligation to ensure that the Article 88 procedure has been complied with, cannot depend on the conduct of the State Authority. If this were the case failure to revoke the decision granting the aid would seriously and adversely affect the Community interest and render practically impossible the recovery required by Community law.</td></tr>
<tr><td colspan="2">The same reasoning applies also for the third question. The beneficiary cannot have a legitimate expectation as to the lawfulness of the aid unless it has been granted in compliance with the procedure of Article 88 EC. Thus, any failure to revoke a decision to grant aid on the basis of the fact that the gain has ceased to exist would render the recovery required by Community law practically impossible. In any case, gain still exists and a beneficiary, who incurs losses after the granting of the aid may however benefit from his temporary survival in terms of retention of market place, reputation and good will.</td></tr>
</table>

APPENDIX XIII
Role of National Courts in the EC System of State Aid Control

Excerpt from *Syndicat Français de l'Express International (SFEI) and Others v La Poste and Others*, (C-39/94, paragraphs 35-53).

"Article 87(1) of the Treaty provides that "(S)ave as otherwise provided in this Treaty, any aid granted by a Member State or through state resources in any form whatsoever which distorts or threatens to distort competition by favouring certain undertakings or the production of certain goods shall, in so far as it affects trade between Member States, be incompatible with the common market."

That prohibition, as a matter of principle, of state aid is neither absolute nor unconditional since paragraph 3 in particular of Article 87 confers on the Commission a wide discretion to allow aid by way of derogation from the general prohibition laid down in paragraph 1 of that article. The determination in such cases of the question whether a state aid is or is not compatible with the common market raises problems which presuppose the examination and appraisal of economic facts and conditions which may be both complex and liable to change rapidly (Case C-301/87, *France v Commission,* 1990 ECR I-307, the "Boussac" case, paragraph 15).

That was the reason for which the Treaty provided in Article 88 for a special procedure under which the Commission would monitor aid schemes and keep them under constant review. With regard to new aid which Member States might be intending to grant, a preliminary procedure was established; if this procedure was not followed, the aid could not be regarded as having been properly granted. By virtue of the first sentence of Article 88(3) of the Treaty, the Commission is to be notified of plans to grant or alter aid before they are put into effect.

The Commission then conducts an initial review of the planned aid. If at the end of that review it considers a plan to be incompatible with the common market, it must without delay initiate the consultative examination procedure under Article 88(2). It follows from the last sentence of Article 88(3) that throughout the preliminary period the Member State concerned may not put the planned aid into effect. Where the consultative examination procedure is initiated, that prohibition continues until the Commission reaches a decision on the compatibility of the planned aid with the common market (see Case C-47/91, *Italy v Commission,* 1992 ECR I-4145, paragraph 24). However, if the Commission has not responded within two months of notification, the Member State concerned may implement the plan after informing the Commission (Case 120/73, *Lorenz v Germany,* 1973 ECR 1471, paragraph 4).

The involvement of national courts is the result of the direct effect which the prohibition on implementation of planned aid laid down in the last sentence of Article 88(3) has been held to have. In this respect, the Court has stated that the immediate applicability of the prohibition on implementation referred to in that article extends to all aid which has been implemented without being notified and, in the event of notification, operates during the preliminary period and if the Commission sets in motion the consultative examination procedure, until the final decision (Case 120/73, *Lorenz,* cited above, paragraph 8, and Case C-354/90, *Fédération Nationale du Commerce Extérieur des Produits Alimentaires and Syndicat National des Négociants et Transformateurs de Saumon,* 1991 ECR I-5505, hereinafter "*FNCE*", paragraph 11).

National courts must offer to individuals the certain prospect that all the appropriate conclusions will be drawn from an infringement of the last sentence of Article 88(3) of the Treaty, in accordance with their national law, as regards the validity of measures giving effect to the aid, the recovery of financial support granted in disregard of that provision and possible interim measures (Case C-354/90, *FNCE,* cited above, paragraph 12).

As regards the supervision of Member States' compliance with their obligations under Articles 87 and 88 of the Treaty, the national courts and the Commission fulfil complementary and separate roles. In drawing the appropriate conclusions from an infringement of the last sentence of Article 88(3), national courts cannot rule on the compatibility of the aid with the common market, that determination being a matter for the Commission, subject to review by the Court of Justice (see Case C-354/90, *FNCE,* cited above, paragraph 14).

Unlike the national courts, the Commission cannot order state aid to be repaid solely on the ground that it has not been notified in accordance with Article 88(3) of the Treaty (see "*Boussac*", cited above, paragraphs 19 to 22, Case C-142/87, *Belgium v Commission,* 1990 ECR I-959, paragraphs 15 to 20 and Case C-354/90, *FNCE,* cited above, paragraph 13). First it must, after giving the Member State in question an opportunity to submit its comments on the matter, issue an interim decision requiring it to suspend immediately the payment of aid pending the outcome of the examination of the aid and to provide the Commission, within such period as it may specify, with all such documentation, information and data as are necessary in order that it may examine the compatibility of the aid with the common market. It is only if the Member State, notwithstanding the Commission's order, fails to provide the information requested that the Commission is empowered to terminate the procedure and make its decision, on the basis of the information available to it, on the question whether or not the aid is compatible with the common market and, if appropriate, call for the recovery of the amount of aid which has already been paid (*"Boussac"*, cited above, paragraphs 19 and 21).

In those circumstances, the initiation by the Commission of a preliminary examination procedure under Article 88(3) or the consultative examination procedure under Article 88(2) cannot release national courts from their duty to safeguard the rights of individuals in the event of a breach of the requirement to give prior notification.

Any other interpretation would have the effect of encouraging the Member States to disregard the prohibition on implementation of planned aid. Since the Commission can do no more than order further payments to be suspended so long as it has not adopted its final decision on the substance of the matter, the effectiveness of Article 88(3) would be weakened if the fact that the Commission was seised of the matter were to prevent the national courts from drawing all the appropriate conclusions from the infringement of that provision.

Similarly, it cannot be accepted that the Commission's delay in completing its preliminary examination may result in the transformation of new aid granted in breach of the last sentence of Article 88(3) of the Treaty into existing aid which can be abolished only with respect to the future.

The Court has, admittedly, held that where a Member State notifies planned measures to the Commission, the latter must decide within two months whether or not to initiate the procedure under Article 88(2). If the Commission does not adopt a decision within that period, the Member State may implement the plan after giving notice to the Commission. The aid is then deemed to be existing aid subject to the review provided for under Article 88(1) and (2) (Case 120/73, *Lorenz v Germany*, cited above, paragraphs 4 and 5).

This case-law is, however, based on the need to take account of the legitimate interest of the Member State in being rapidly informed of the legal position. That element is missing where the Member State has implemented planned aid without having notified the Commission beforehand.

Finally, a national court may have cause to interpret the concept of aid contained in Article 87 of the Treaty in order to determine whether a state measure introduced without observance of the preliminary examination procedure provided for in Article 88(3) ought to have been subject to that procedure (Case 78/76, *Steinike und Weinlig v Germany*, 1977 ECR 595, paragraph 14, and Case C-189/91, *Kirsammer-Hack v Sidal*, 1993 ECR I-6185, paragraph 14).

Where the national court entertains doubts as to whether the measures at issue should be categorised as state aid, it may seek clarification from the Commission on that point. In its notice on cooperation between national courts and the Commission in the state aid field (OJ C 312, 23/11/1995), the Commission expressly encouraged national courts to make contact with it when they encounter difficulties in the application of Article 88(3) of the Treaty and explained what kind of information it was able to supply. It should be noted, in that regard, that as a consequence of the duty of sincere cooperation between the Community institutions and the Member States resulting from Article 5 of the Treaty (Case C-2/88, *Imm. Zwartveld and Others*, 1990 I-3365, paragraphs 17 and 18), the Commission must respond as quickly as possible to requests from national courts.

Moreover, in accordance with the second and third paragraphs of Article 234 of the Treaty, the national court may or must request the Court for a preliminary ruling on the interpretation of Article 87 of the Treaty.

Where it is likely that some time will elapse before it gives its final judgment, it is for the national court to decide whether it is necessary to order interim relief such as the suspension of the measures at issue in order to safeguard the interests of the parties.

A national court, seised of a request that it should draw the appropriate conclusions from an infringement of the last sentence of Article 88(3) of the Treaty, where the matter has also been referred to the Commission, which has not yet given a final decision as to whether the state measures constitute state aid, is not required to declare that it lacks jurisdiction or to stay proceedings until such time as the Commission has adopted a position on how the measures in question are to be categorised. With a view to determining whether those measures should have been notified to the Commission, a national court may have cause to interpret and apply the concept of aid. In case of doubt, it may ask the Commission for clarification. Furthermore, it may or must, in accordance with the second and third paragraphs of Article 234 of the Treaty, refer a question to the Court of Justice for a preliminary ruling. Where it consults the Commission or refers a question to the Court, it must decide whether it is necessary to order interim measures in order to safeguard the interests of the parties pending final judgment."

INTERNATIONAL COMPETITION LAW SERIES

1. Ignacio De León, *Latin American Competition Law and Policy: A Policy in Search of Identity* (2001)
(ISBN 90-411-1542-0)

2. Wim Dejonghe and Wouter Van de Voorde (Eds.), *M & A in Belgium* (2001)
(ISBN 90-411-1594-3)

3. Yang-Ching Chao, Gee San, Changfa Lo, Jiming Ho (Eds.), *International and Comparative Competition Law and Policies* (2001)
(ISBN 90-411-1643-5)

4. Martin Mendelsohn and Stephen Rose, *Guide to the EC Block Exemption for Vertical Agreements* (2002)
(ISBN 90-411-9813-X)

5. Clifford A. Jones and Mitsuo Matsushita (Eds.), *Competition Policy in the Global Trading System* (2002)
(ISBN 90-411-1758-X)

6. Christian Koenig, Andreas Bartosch, Jens-Daniel Braun (Eds.), *EC Competition and Telecommunications Law* (2002)
(ISBN 90-411-1814-4)

7. Jürgen Basedow (Ed.), *Limits and Control of Competition with a View to International Harmonization* (2002)
(ISBN 90-411-1967-1)

8. Maureen Brunt, *Economic Essays on Australian and New Zealand Competition Law* (2003)
(ISBN 90-411-1991-4)

9. Ky P. Ewing, Jr., *Competition Rules for the 21st Century: Principles from America's Experience* (2003)
(ISBN 90-411-2006-8)

10. Joseph Wilson, *Globalization and the Limits of National Merger Control Laws* (2003)
(ISBN 90-411-1996-5)

11. Peter Verloop and Valérie Landes (Eds.), *Merger Control in Europe, 4th edition, EU, Member States and Accession States* (2003)
(ISBN 90-411-2056-4)

12. Themistoklis, K. Giannakopoulos, *Safeguarding Companies' Rights in Competition and Anti-dumping/Anti-subsidies Proceedings* (2004)
(ISBN 90-411-2254-0)

13. Marjorie Holmes and Lesley Davey (Eds.), *A Practical Guide to National Competition Rules across Europe* (2004)
(ISBN 90-411-2295-8)

14. Sigrid Stroux, *US and EU Oligopoly Control* (2004)
(ISBN 90-411-2296-6)

15. Tzong-Leh Hwang and Chiyuan Chen (Eds.), *The Future Development of Competition Framework* (2004)
(ISBN 90-411-2305-9)

16. Phedon Nicolaides, Mihalis Kekelekis and Philip Buyskes, *State Aid Policy in the European Community. A Guide for Practitioners* (2005)
(ISBN 90-411-2394-6)